Annotated Bibliography on Childhood, with Emphasis on Africa: Outline, General Findings and Research Recommendations

Patti Henderson

Monograph Series

CODESRIA

Annotated Bibliography on Childhood, with Emphasis on Africa: Outline, General Findings and Research Recommendations

Patti Henderson
Department of Social Anthropology
University of Cape Town

Monograph Series

The **CODESRIA Monograph Series** is published to stimulate debate, comments, and further research on the subjects covered. The Series will serve as a forum for works based on the findings of original research, which however are too long for academic journals but not long enough to be published as books, and which deserve to be accessible to the research community in Africa and elsewhere. Such works may be case studies, theoretical debates or both, but they incorporate significant findings, analyses, and critical evaluations of the current literature on the subjects in question.

**Annotated Bibliography on Childhood, with Emphasis on Africa:
Outline, General Findings and Research Recommendations**

Typeset by CODESRIA
Printed by Lightning Source

ISBN: 2-86978-119-9
ISBN-13: 978-2-86978-119-1

CODESRIA would like to express its gratitude to the Swedish International
Development Cooperation Agency (Sida/SAREC), the International Development
Research Centre (IDRC), the Ford Foundation, the Mac Arthur Foundation,
Carnegie Corporation, the Norwegian Ministry of Foreign Affairs, the Danish
Agency for International Development (DANIDA), the French Ministry of
Cooperation, the Rockefeller Foundation, the United Nations Development
Programme (UNDP), The Netherlands Ministry of Foreign Affairs, the
Government of Senegal, FINIDA, NORAD, CIDA, IIEP/ADEA, OECD, IFS,
Oxfam America UN/UNICEF, for their support of its research, training and
publications programmes.

Contents

Outline

The annotated bibliography presented below is constructed from recent literature on children and childhood, published between 1995 and 2000, with emphasis on Africa. It includes some relevant theoretical texts and studies from other parts of the world. As child studies and the idea of childhood are a broad area of investigation, the bibliography makes no claim to be representative of all the new developments in the field. There is emphasis on anthropological, sociological and psychological literature. A few contributors from Economics and Political Science are included.

Societal constructions of childhood have begun to unravel globally, and particularly in post-colonial Africa, because of an irreconcilable gap between the ways in which adults think about childhood in relation to social ideals, and the ways in which children live and act in contradistinction to these conceptions. In many writings on childhood, children are portrayed as needing adult protection and as occupying a transitional social space on the road to adulthood. The idea of children in need of protection, in their capacity as passive recipients of socialisation processes, is challenged by the recognition of their responsibilities and agency, and their participation in activities that counter conceptions about childhood as a period of innocence set apart from unpalatable realities. Children's participation in war constitutes one of the challenges to adult conceptions about social order.

On the other hand, the marginalisation of many, but not all youths, in Africa, is marked in terms of their exclusion from access to mainstream political and social power, and economic processes. The lack of access to social, political, and economic resources among youths does not allow for their smooth transition to the approved roles of adulthood. Attempts to block youths' access to the markers of adulthood may undermine their sense of personality, as these markers point to an achieved personhood associated with the accoutrements of adulthood. Given the ways in which children challenge notions of childhood and youths are often blocked in the transition to adulthood, the idea of childhood and the social category of youth begin to blur into one another. Children take on the imagined characteristics of older people through their actions as youths assume features purportedly pertaining to "children". It is for this reason that reference is made to some studies concerning youth in Africa in the annotated bibliography.

Books and articles referred to in the annotated bibliography should be read in conjunction with an annotated bibliography compiled for CODESRIA by Fiona Ross, who covered childhood studies prior to 1995. Overviews of two recent conferences on youth in Africa are given at the end of the annotated bibliography. The proceedings of the conferences are to be worked into forthcoming publications and should greatly contribute to a body of literature on children and youth in Africa. A list of references (un-annotated) is presented, as it will be of interest to child studies specialists in Africa – at least in revealing, in some instances, how children's lives are rendered invisible. A review of on-line resources covering childhood issues on the Internet is beyond the scope of the study and constitutes an area for further research. Some of the articles placed on the Web are not necessarily "published" in any other form. I have included a few on-line addresses relevant to child studies in the list of additional references at the end of the bibliography.

Findings

In undertaking child studies, a seemingly obvious distinction should be made between children and childhood. Studies often portray abstract ideas about children that fail to reflect their views and actions. Children, their lives and imaginings may be rendered invisible if overlaid with visions of their place in society. Although in many theoretical approaches to child studies there is emphasis on the need to consult children themselves and acknowledge their agency in shaping society, few studies have paid children the respect they deserve by working directly and constantly with them.

Children exist everywhere, but they negotiate different terrains of childhood. The experience of childhood differs in varying localities and is shaped by class, cultural conceptions, social power, gender, race, age, nationality and economic systems. It is, therefore, pertinent not to speak of childhood as a unitary conception.

The recognition of differing contexts and parameters of childhood cannot be glibly proclaimed. If we are to improve the lives of children or to recognise their active contribution to societies in terms of practice and imaginative constructions of the future, we have to avoid resorting too quickly to existing categories in which to place children's understanding.

A unitary conception of childhood emerges from within a modernist framework peculiar to Western discourses and disciplines. These disciplines, until very recently, have borne the traces of Enlightenment thought through which universal knowledge claims are made. It is not always transparent that a particular model of childhood predominant in wealthy industrialised countries and bearing little relation even to the realities of those countries can define research parameters in different social contexts. Once specific conceptions about childhood, child development and the status of children are overturned in academic discourse, worn-out conceptions continue to "haunt" the practice of institutions directly affecting the lives of children in many parts of the world, often to their detriment. Conceptions that adhere to mythic and sentimental views of childhood are absorbed into institutional *doxa* (Bourdieu and Eagleton 1994)[1] — the institutionalised habitual ways in which individuals interacting with children and their guardians come to limit the possibilities of care, to impose what is appropriate for a child to do, and to set normative standards as to what constitutes a family. Welfare, including legal, medical, military, educational and psychological practices, often linked with the nation-state or with international Non Governmental Organisations (NGOs), entails assumptions regarding children (as do parents). Mechanisms of the daily practice of institutions linked to the state and NGOs seem to require a formulaic gathering or presentation of information that fails to capture the fluidity and dexterity of children's lives and may indeed misrepresent them. Misrepresentation results in a misfit between policies directed towards children and the varying realities in which they live. Policies are faulty because they are based on misconceptions upheld as universal realities. Notions of universality foreclose an intellectual space in which the specificity of local models of childhood as well as the varying realities of individual children's lives in local contexts can be seriously considered. Ironically, in countries where the nation-state has lost its legitimacy, and where the majority of people live around the margins of diminishing state influence — whose only effective trace may be a monopoly of access to resources and the infliction of terror — the reality of children's lives, the details of their trials, social contributions and their imaginative

---

[1] Bourdieu, P. & T. Eagleton, 1994, Doxa and Common Life: An Interview, pp.265-77, in S. Zizek, *Mapping Ideology*, London, New York, Verso.

3

reach are often missed[2]. The bulk of research on children in Africa is conducted under the auspices of large international organisations such as the United Nations Children's Fund (UNICEF), the World Health Organisation (WHO) and the International Labour Organisation (ILO). Organisations like those above demand a degree of standardisation in producing knowledge for comparative research. However, the categories that come to define globalised areas of research across multiple social contexts often fail to create the kind of knowledge that propels understandings beyond existing homilies. Researchers may succumb to the numbing effect of circulatory teleological notions that fail to render fresh approaches to the study of children and childhood.

A few categories that need to be critically examined within the African context (and elsewhere) include, for example, child labour, child soldiers, and youth[3]. Many of the studies mentioned in the annotated bibliography either espouse these categories uncritically or begin to question their validity. The studies that utilise these categories uncritically, in addition to contributing to the circulation of tired ideas as stated above, contribute to the ways in which youth and children are pathologised and cast as anti-social. Bald accounts of children are unable to hold the fine-grained ways in which children and youths lead complex lives that simultaneously intermingle both "the good" and "the bad".

The idea of "child labour" arises from an impassioned attempt to universalise Western conceptions of childhood and a notion that children should be excluded from all forms of work. The bid to prevent children from working reveals an understanding of children as passive and dependent recipients of adult nurturing. It makes invisible some of the attributes of children that are imbued with effective personhood. It fails to foreground invisible forms of child work, for example, in homes and family

---

[2] Filip De Boeck's work (1999) on Zairean youth mining diamonds in the border regions of Angola provides one exception to the failure to describe young people's lives in volatile social contexts. His work is referred to in the conference section of the bibliography.

[3] The idea of the 'best interests of the child' is another example of 'shorthand' phrase frequently used in discourses on childhood. The content or meaning of the phrase has seldom been developed coherently and the way it is used by default constitutes a protective device whereby relevant decisions and policies are screened from probing questions.

enterprises. Likewise, romanticisation of children as social beings set apart from the exigencies of adult life fails to recognise them as agents in society and as contributors of value to economic processes. The recognition of many children's contribution to their own survival and the survival of their families is therefore undercut. Children's work is pathologised, as are the ways in which many people in poor countries survive. In places where children's work is vital for the survival of not only children but of their families, and where work is an important prerequisite for self-worth and the development of personhood, insisting that children do not work may undercut whole social systems. Researchers have come to understand that the meanings and value of child work differ across a variety of social and cultural contexts. It is predominantly anthropological studies (Nieuwenhys 1996) that have opened up recognition of new areas of exploitation (unpaid work) and an appreciation for the positive aspects of child income-generating activities in many contexts across the globe. Detailed studies have resulted in some revision of global policies concerning child work and children's rights.

The "child soldier" category contains the emotive inflection of distaste, a moral condemnation similar to the one enshrined in the idea of "child labour". The active participation of young children as combatants in many of Africa's (and other) contemporary wars has resulted in a generalised fear of popular appeal for ordered society. The idea of "child soldier" reflects a sense that the phenomenon of children in war can only be explained by casting them as unwilling victims of forced recruitment processes. While it is true that many children (both boys and girls) are forcibly incorporated into armed militia, the discourse on child soldiering often fails to recognise children's conscious and principled decision to enter armed conflicts for ideological reasons (for example, to confront oppressive regimes, as in Apartheid South Africa). Children may consciously become participants in armed conflict to protect parents and/or to contribute to others' and their own survival. More subtle attention must be paid to gender considerations in situations of armed conflict. On the one hand, the political role of girls in turbulent contexts is often downplayed in matters concerning child soldiering. On the other hand, although girls are often described as giving auxiliary support, and as "war wives" in contexts of war, the predominant focus of study is often on how boys are incorporated into armed forces as combatants.

The possibility of setting children in any war apart from the horrors and changing social circumstances engendered by war remains questionable. As "ideal" notions of the space of childhood are inverted, whereas this entails a threat to visions of society, the erosion of innocence implied by the idea of child soldier creates an opposing conception of children as demonic and dangerous. In isolating the notion of child soldiers, researchers seem to elide adult responsibility and incorporation into wars and their horrors. In pathologising child soldiers, attention is deflected from the ways in which adult society has failed children and contributed to war. Preoccupation with child soldiering in many cases also deflects attention from the systemic violence of many societies in times of peace. The insertion of violence into life through economic strictures, for example, is ignored. (Lutz and Nonini 1999[4] and Henderson 1999, see annotated bibliography).

The category of "youth", particularly in Africa, denotes preoccupation with young people as marginalised from mainstream political, economic and social practices. The notion of youth has become salient in Africa predominantly in describing the slippage of underemployed and criminalised young men into gangs or armed militia. In recent thinking, youths are associated with global forms of desire for access to resources and commodities. (This is not really a new idea as youths have always been cultural brokers between the old and the new; see below). The limitations of the way in which the idea of youth is being used in contemporary studies consist in the fact that scant attention is paid to young people who try to fulfil responsibilities, create jobs and hold families together, despite the difficulties facing them. When global processes are linked with conceptions of youth (for example, the world-wide dissemination of certain forms of youth culture), the diversity of young people in Africa is often underestimated in drawing attention to an assumed homogeneity. Young women and girls are on the whole startlingly absent from serious studies concerning youth. In cases young women and girls are mentioned, they often represent victims of the violent circumstances prevailing in some African countries. Girls may become hypnotic ciphers of the experience of rape, for example. Although terror inflicted by and on young people should be seriously considered, I question the circulation of particular obsessions and lack of imaginative

---

[4] See C. Lutz & D. Nonini, 1999. "The Violence of Economies and the Economies of Violence", pp. 73-113, in H. Moore (ed.) *Anthropological Theory Today*, London, Polity Press.

reach in describing a range of experience. In addition to the above criticism of ways in which youths are being considered, a focus on youth is accompanied by a widespread lack of serious attention to the study of young children.

There are difficulties in writing on areas of childhood dealing with violence, silence, and predicting outcomes. An erroneous conception common in the literature is that children who have undergone extreme hardship will necessarily perpetuate anti-social and violent acts. In relation to the problem of writing violence, respect and care for children need to be demonstrated. Valentine Daniel (1996) [5] has outlined a dual approach in writing violence. It is important to disaggregate and contextualise various forms of violence. On the other hand, there is a sense in which the effects of violence are beyond articulation. Daniels suggests that we hold the above paradox in dynamic tension in our attempts to write violence. The hypnotic focussing on violent events may contribute to a kind of pornographic voyeurism, especially if the "voices" of recipients of violence are not contextualised, and especially if they are children with little access to public discourse on setting right the ways in which others portray them. Subtle work has been done in this area by Veena Das (1996, see also Henderson 1994 and 1999) [6].

One consequence of framing child studies within inadequate categories evincing a narrow topicality and alarm is that the integration of children and childhood in dense structures of history and time is missed. Few African studies are exemplary in locating children within cosmologies linked with ancestral forebears that change the ways in which we are able to "think" about suffering and affliction (Reynolds 1996). Some writers are beginning to describe the complexities of people's responses to experiences of social dislocation within frameworks suggested by cosmologies. For

---

[5] Valentine Daniel, E., 1996, *Charred Lullabies: Chapters in an Anthropography of Violence*, Princeton, Princeton University Press.

[6] Das, V., 1996. Language and the Body: Transactions in the Construction of Pain. *Daedelus*, vol. 125(1): 67-91; Henderson, P., 1994. Silence, Sex and Authority: The construction of young girls' sexuality in New Crossroads, Cape Town. *Women and Autonomy Journal (VENA)*, vol. 6(2): 33-39; Henderson, P., 1999, see annotated bibliography.

example, Hylton White, Alcinda Honwana and Bridgitte Bagnol[7] are exploring ways in which the living, in relationship with the dead, are able to repair — through ritual — rents within the social fabric, and injury to personhood. The physical, social and moral afflictions suffered by the living are attributable to anti-social actions, not only of the living, but also of the dead. Social suffering, therefore, links generations of people and marks complex forms of social responsibility. Through recognition of ancestors' social omissions, the living are able to reconfigure the social world on their behalf. The living too are aware that their actions have long-term consequences for their descendants. Despite people's experience of war and fragmentation, they continue to uphold visions of social coherence and social goals that may be acted upon in collective ways that defy the location of suffering or its cure within the individual.

I have shown how children are generally credited with very little power, among other things, through the use of limited categories to encompass their experience. Children have power and agency but these attributes receive scant recognition in public life. Such shortcomings call for commitment to a different vision of power and citizenship, one that includes children. Two contemporary developments may well force adults to re-conceptualise the ways in which children and childhood have thus far been described, and may force a space where children's power is recognised. These are, on the one hand, the advent of AIDS, and, on the other hand, new developments in information technology. Prevalent notions of the authority of adulthood may be reshaped by the fact that many very young people will be the majority of survivors in places where the AIDS pandemic results in widespread deaths of productive men and women. It will often devolve on youths to devise ways of constituting forms of sociability, responsibility and the protection of younger children. In the context of Africa, young people, especially migrants, have always been the bearers of innovation, bringing to their homes new forms of technology

---

[7] Hylton White is completing a doctorate in social anthropology at the University of Chicago. His work considers repair and reconfiguration of social relationships centred in rural homes in KwaZulu/Natal, South Africa. Alcinda Honwana has written on ritual healing for children in Mozambique and Angola (see annotated bibliography). Bridgitte Bagnol is a doctoral student in social anthropology at the University of Cape Town. Her work deals with the social relationships brought into being through bride-wealth transactions in Maputo, Mozambique.

(for example, agricultural equipment, new musical instruments, etc.)[8]. The young are no less responsive in commandeering information technology. However, whereas some earlier innovations required little capital outlay, and were easily transported to rural areas, the same cannot be said for information technology that is not only expensive but also requires electricity. Among the minority of people who have access to contemporary information technology, the young often supersede parents and caretakers in the range of their knowledge and competency, and in their easy adoption of rapidly changing electronic communication networks. In their dexterity, children may out-leap their guardians and come to create surprising and fluid social boundaries that change the ways in which we think of life courses from birth through childhood and adulthood to death.

Recommendations

Despite the ways in which international organisations and academic disciplines set the agenda for researching children and childhood in Africa, ways must be found to enrich the study of children. One mechanism consists in facilitating systematic studies in diverse African contexts, an approach aimed at creating, while acknowledging global processes and their localised appropriation, what Jo Boyden has called "a base-line of data concerning children in Africa". (Paul Richards' book on youth and war in Sierra Leone (1996) has for instance been criticised for lacking ethnographic data. See below). The truth is that few studies on children in Africa evoke the lives of children in detailed and nuanced ways. In a too easy capitulation to categories with global circulation, and in the researchers' haste to describe trends in post-colonial Africa, we may miss important areas of children's worlds and produce a body of work proclaiming a set of uninspiring generalisations. A fixation with "fashionable" ideas may result in beautifully written studies which, on closer examination, lack data accuracy and depth. The challenge is, therefore, to write well and imaginatively while paying sufficient attention to data production. In most African social contexts, scarcity, inequitable power relations, diverse forms of violence, suffering and innovation militate against neglecting to pay attention to

---

[8] For examples of the young as brokers between the old and the new, see De Boeck, 1999; Ngwane, 1999 & Wolputte, 1999 in the conference section of the annotated bibliography.

9

detail. A post-modern and apolitical preoccupation with the irrelevance of truths is increasingly difficult to uphold with equanimity, even in social contexts where resources and ideas circulate in relatively equitable ways.

In order to produce diverse and telling studies on children, innovative methodological approaches should be devised in writing on the ways in which children live and contribute to the re-figuring of society. Examples of innovative methodological approaches to the study of childhood are included in the works of certain writers mentioned in the bibliography (see, for example, Nieuwenhys 1994, in Fiona Ross' annotated bibliography; Reynolds 1996; Goldman 1998, and Henderson 1999).

It is perhaps expedient to begin questioning the very notion of child studies as, theoretically and ethnographically, writers in the field have come up with very little that is new in recent years. The idea of child studies should be critically examined in the same way as women's studies. The universal category of women has been effectively undermined by the insistence on difference between and amongst women. We have scarcely discussed the various aspects of childhood in social and cultural contexts in different parts of the world. One of the reasons is perhaps that children are not granted any acknowledged power in many societies. If we take on the task of describing the contextualised ways in which children live, noting the particular intersections of local and global influences and exchange in children's lives, we will begin to think beyond the categories that at present confine our understanding.

Bibliography of Children

Abdullah, I., 1997. "Bush Path to Destruction: The Origin and Character of the Revolutionary United Front (RUF/L)". *Africa Development*, vol. 22(3/4): 46-76

Ibrahim Abdullah's article on the Revolutionary United Front (RUF) provides a critique of Paul Richards' romanticised account of the recent war in Sierra Leone (1996, see below in the annotated bibliography). Abdullah examines the lumpen cultural base of groups of young people who began war in the hinterland in Kailahun District in March 1991. Youth commanders from the same base seized power in a coup d'état in Freetown, the capital city, twelve months later. "Both events were products of a rebellious youth culture in search of a viable alternative —without a concrete agenda — to the bankrupt All Peoples Congress (APC) regime" (p.46). The absence of a well-conceived radical alternative to the old regime led, in the writer's view, to the subsequent escalation of war and infliction of terror by the RUF on the civilian population. Abdullah traces the demise of a radical tradition in post-independence Sierra Leone and a concomitant marginalisation of youth organisations. By the late 1970s the APC had entrenched itself and suppressed all opposition.

Abdullah criticises Richards' use of the trope of the forest and its resources as an explanatory framework for youth involvement in the RUF bush war. In contrast, the writer emphasises the long history of rebellious youth culture in Sierra Leone as constituting the bedrock of youth militancy. This youth culture emerged in the 1940s amongst lumpen male youths (sometimes referred to as *rarray* boys) who were mostly uneducated second-generation residents of Sierra Leonean cities. *Rarray* boys soon came to play the role of thugs for politicians who sought to enforce their positions. The 1970s marked the incorporation of middle-class youth into the cultural activities of lumpen youths. Abdullah traces the influence of reggae music, Fela Kuti's politicised lyrics, and Gaddafi's *Green Book* on Sierra Leonean youth. (Abdullah's critique of Gaddafi's *Green Book* is that it promulgates populist ideas lacking in considered political analysis. In addition it espouses a naive form of Pan Africanism). In the late 1970s and 1980s, students who embraced the lumpen rebellious youth culture centring on the *pote* (informal drinking places) led demonstrations. The writer explains the lack of maturity in youth politics in terms of lack of coherent radical tradition and adoption of an uncritical Pan Africanism by youths.

Subsequently, the RUF (that drew its supporters from marginalised youth culture) was responsible for the terror inflicted on the population they claimed to be liberating. The RUF did not share the characteristics of other revolutionary movements in terms of coherent ideology, organisational structure or codes of discipline.

Bangura, Y., 1997. "Understanding the Political and Cultural Dynamics of the Sierra Leone War: A Critique of Paul Richards' Fighting for the Rain Forest", *Africa Development*, vol. 22(3/4): 117-35

In a brief overview of Yusuf Bangura's response to Paul Richards' Book on youth and war in Sierra Leone, I concentrate on the critique concerning claims about youth. Paul Richards' book appears in summarised form in the annotated bibliography. Bangura takes issue with Richards in response to his attempt to portray the role of the Revolutionary United Front (RUF) in Sierra Leone's six-year war as rational, as demonstrating a coherent political programme, and as being led by young revolutionary intellectuals.

He argues that Richards does not examine in any depth the historical origins of the RUF or the peculiarities of the governing party at that time. the All Peoples Congress (APC). Bangura holds a position contrary to that of Richards, who argued that the failure of the State in Sierra Leone was linked to a decrease in patrimonial relations within the State structures. In contrast, Bangura shows evidence that the State failure was rather due to an unprecedented increase in patrimonial relations among State officials to the detriment of public institutions. The State began to relinquish its responsibilities to citizens, for example, by relying on donor agencies to provide welfare and educational facilities for the majority of the population.

According to Bangura, Richards' analysis of youth culture in Sierra Leone is weak and that his conclusions about youth participation in the war are not always reliable. Richards gathered data from young people living in urban areas and not from RUF combatants. Bangura suggests that it is methodologically erroneous to attribute the views of urban youth to RUF combatants. Conclusions that cast all young people in Sierra Leone in the same mould overlook differences between them. Referring to Richards. Bangura writes:

> He is unable to distinguish between the strata of youth that are often called "lumpens", or "*rarray man dem*" in popular discourse, who are believed to be the driving force of the RUF's fighting machine, and other types of youth who, although disadvantaged, remain socially integrated into community and family institutions that guarantee social accountability (p.120).

Bangura suggests that Richards inadvertently "glorifies" the atrocities of the RUF in his efforts to disprove the new barbarism' thesis promulgated by the American Journalist, Kaplan, as an explanatory framework in which contemporary wars in Africa are described as predominantly anarchic. Although Bangura commends Richards in his description of the difficulties facing contemporary youths in Sierra Leone, he stresses that the vast majority of youths are anti-RUF. Unlike youths with loosely structured working relations and family life, who formed the majority of RUF cadres, the majority of youths sustain life as traders, artisans. farmers, apprentices. labourers, workers, tailors, dancers, dramatists, domestic and office helpers etc. (p.140). Bangura argues that the RUF was not a revolutionary movement in the classic sense and that it is dangerous to downplay the terror the RUF inflicted on the population by stressing the rational aspects of the RUF movement. Terror viewed as a post-modern form of communication with the outside world is, in Bangura's view, naive and irresponsible. Bangura points out that rationality and terror are not mutually exclusive. Many rational systems have been highly successful in inflicting terror on enemies and their rationalism does not mitigate their actions.

Brett, R. and M. McCallin, 1996, *Children, The Invisible Soldiers,* Geneva, Radda Barnen, 257 pp, including Index and Useful Bibliography on Children, ISBN: 91-88726-56-8.

The book grew out of collaboration between a number of organisations across the world and the United Nations Study of the Impact of Armed Conflict on Children (the Machel Study, see below). Information is compiled from 26 country case studies including the African countries of Burundi, Ethiopia, Liberia, Mozambique, Rwanda, South Africa and Uganda. (Detailed individual case studies do not feature in the book but are available on request from Radda Barnen's Project on Child Soldiers, Radda Barnen, 10788, Stockholm, Sweden, e-mail al.andrews@baf.rb.se.)

The book includes tables and maps that are limited, however, by a general lack of reliable documentation on child soldiers.

The authors suggest that the recruitment of children into armies is more pervasive than realised. When soldiers are needed, especially in situations of civil war, children are often more easily recruited than adults. Children may be press-ganged into armies by both governmental and opposition forces. They may volunteer to join a particular armed grouping in search of physical and economic security and for cultural and ideological reasons. One main reason why children volunteer for oppositional groupings is their own experience of ill-treatment by governmental forces, the death of their family members, destruction of their homes, and the torture they themselves undergo.

The book asserts that child soldiers come from the poorest and most marginalised sectors of society. Those who are most vulnerable are children without families, with no access to education or a reasonable standard of living, and those living within conflict zones. Little systematic evidence is given in support of the above claim.

A global overview of child soldiering is presented. It is estimated that a quarter of a million children under the age of eighteen are involved in governmental and opposition forces across the globe. The writers state that child soldiers are often invisible because those who employ them deny their existence. Children's direct participation in armed forces is, however, not new. The book touches on the issue of gender, suggesting that boys and men are predominantly involved in armed combat in both governmental and oppositional forces and that women and girls provide a vast army of support and ancillary workers. Where girls are involved as combatants, they usually constitute members of oppositional forces. In Ethiopia, for example, women and girls form 20 to 25 percent of the oppositional force. Girls incorporated or conscripted into armed forces are often sexually exploited by men and boys and become the war "wives" of soldiers. In addition to providing sex for soldiers, girls are required to cook and wash clothes.

The book deals with recruitment of child soldiers. Questionnaires issued in the 26 countries distinguished between compulsory, forced, voluntary and induced recruitment. The writers argue that the ways in which boys and girls become part of armed forces is often unknown and that the categories of recruitment defined in the questionnaire are sometimes blurred in real life. The existence of conscription with a legal minimum age is no guarantee against the recruitment of child soldiers in government forces. Recruiters required to provide soldiers in terms of quotas often make up the shortfall with underage recruits, for example, in Ethiopia. Indirect conscription through local authorities is open to manipulation, substitution and corruption. Many governmental and oppositional forces are involved in forced recruitment. Children are approached on the street, in market places, on their way to school, while playing or selling on the street, at school and at home. Often children are abducted during attacks on villages. Sometimes children volunteer by proxy, hoping to release a family member from the army or from jail. Children (and youths) are often involved in local militias; for example, in South Africa, youths protected their neighbourhoods whilst fighting against the apartheid state.

Cairns, E. (ed.), 1996. *Children and Political Violence*, Cambridge, Mass, Blackwell, 219 pp, including Index, ISBN: 1-55786-351-2

This book is a comparative review and critique of research literature on the effects of political violence on children. The author contextualises children's participation in and experience of political violence and avoids "over-psychologising" violent behaviour. Because children have been invisible socially it has been presumed that they do not participate in or suffer from the effects of social conflict. This is patently not the case. Cairns therefore decries the lack of writing on the experience of children in situations like the Holocaust. The book brings together information from disparate sources to evaluate the impact of political violence on child aggression, moral development and interpersonal relationships. Data on the psychological effects of political violence on children are available from few countries.

The countries named by Cairns include South Africa, Israel, Lebanon and Northern Ireland. Little research has been done on the psychological effects of violence on children in Latin America and the rest of Africa.

In Cairns' view, ideas concerning children and political violence are social constructions and therefore difficult to define. The author writes against a universalised model of child development, suggesting that childhood, adolescence and adulthood are socially defined status including expectations that differ across cultural and social domains. Such differences are important to consider when defining child symptoms and their participation in political movements. Children's experience in different contexts of war may not necessarily be comparable or identical (p.166). Children's evaluation of violence may change in different contexts. They may positively evaluate violence undertaken in the name of a legitimate cause and may decry violence that appears to be of no purpose. Violence is therefore construed differently and experienced less negatively at different historical moments.

Cairns shows how the literature on children and political violence is dominated by what psychologists have termed "stress" and "copying mechanisms". The underlying assumption is that every child exposed to political violence will necessarily suffer serious psychological consequences. Chapter Two of the book implies that suffering is not inevitable. There is a tendency to apply the criteria of Post-Traumatic Stress Disorder (PTSD) to children who do suffer although they display a wide and variable range of symptoms. No clear conclusions can be made as to why certain children are more resilient than others in terms of their experience of political violence. In studies where variables like age, sex, personality are demarcated as possible contributory factors of children's resilience or lack thereof, they tend to be considered in isolation.

Cairns stresses the need for detailed studies of children's social support networks including the extended family, peers and the wider community in evaluating their experience of political violence. There is a weakness in the methodology of assessing child psychological health, as investigations are confined in most cases to biological parents, often mothers, when it comes to gleaning information. There is little information on how children evaluate different forms of violence, on how children obtain information about on-going political violence or on their coping strategies in contexts of political violence. The impact of political violence should not only be confined to psychological issues but must encompass its effects on the material support to children.

Cairns suggests that the long-term effects of political violence should not be evaluated in one-off studies. Instead, the effects of stress should be considered as part of an on-going process of person-situation interaction over time. Future research should incorporate an understanding of children's social identities, of the groups with whom children identify as these may influence whether an act of political violence is viewed positively or negatively. It is therefore incorrect to argue that children will necessarily perpetuate their experiences of violence in a negative way in their future relations with others. There is no evidence that political violence has an impact on moral reasoning and therefore it cannot be argued that children who have been involved in political conflict will automatically become linked to anti-social acts and crime when political conflict has ended. Children's ability to engage intelligently and socially with trauma has been underestimated. Cairns concludes that psychological approaches to the study of children in political conflict have paid more attention to decontextualised individuals than to groups, communities and socio-political factors.

Clapham, C. (ed.), 1998, *African Guerrillas*, Oxford, Kampala, Bloomington and Indianapolis, James Currey, Fountain Publishers, Indiana University Press.

Christopher Clapham's book provides a useful background to understanding war in contemporary Africa and is an important complement to Radda Barnen's book on child soldiers. The book features studies by a variety of academics on the history and meaning of particular armed conflicts in Eritrea, Tigray, Sudan, Somalia, Uganda, Rwanda, Democratic Republic of Congo (DRC), Liberia and Sierra Leone.

In the preface to the book, Clapham suggests that groups across the continent resorted to war in pursuit of state power and economic and spiritual goals as the institutional infrastructure of African states lacked efficacy and legitimacy. Armed insurrections in the countryside and military coups by state personnel characterise some of the conflicts. Case studies provided in the book begin to address the need for serious analysis of the differences and variety of conflicts across tropical Africa from the Horn through Central Africa to coastal West Africa. The authors are at pains to describe the particularity and varied conditions resulting in different armed movements. The study therefore warns against the dangers of excessive generalisation.

Cosaro, W. A., 1997, *The Sociology of Childhood*. Thousand Oaks, California, London, New Delhi, Pine Forge Press, 304 pp., ISBN: 0-8039-9011-1.

William Cosaro argues that sociology has a limited tradition with regard to the study of childhood. Until recently, childhood was marginal in sociological studies. Childhood and children were accommodated within theoretical frameworks shaped by notions of socialisation, families and education. The theoretical underpinnings of the frameworks suggested that childhood was a transitional phase in which children gained cumulative knowledge of the social world, approached and entered adulthood through the acquisition of various competencies. The latter views have been described elsewhere as constituting a deficit model of childhood. New theoretical and empirical trends stress the conceptual autonomy of children and childhood. There is now greater emphasis on children's relationships, apart from those they have with adults, for example, and with their peers. Interpretative perspectives have been adopted in examining the lives of children that overturn assumptions contained in theories of socialisation.

Cosaro insists on two principles in guiding research on children and childhood. Firstly, children must be viewed as social agents in their own right and, secondly, childhood should be viewed as a structural form within society, and accorded the status of social categories such as class, age and gender.

Eleven chapters span four sections of the book. Part One reviews traditional approaches to socialisation and child development in sociology and psychology. Cosaro shows how the idea of children's passivity emerged from behaviourist models of child development that were later challenged by constructivist models of development psychology: those created, for example, by Piaget and Vygotsky. Cosaro suggests that children actively contribute to societal reproduction as well as to change. Part Two provides a historical and cultural review of classic work on the history of childhood. Drawing on historical records of children in America and in other societies, Cosaro shows how children have contributed to societal production and change, creating their own child cultures. In some industrialised and developing societies, children and childhood are examined cross-culturally by investigating families and social change. Part Three explores the importance of children's peer cultures to a new sociology of childhood. Peer cultures are examined in terms of their symbolic and material attributes. Control, communal sharing, autonomy, self and identity are highlighted as important areas for study within children's peer cultures. Part Four deals with ideological notions that cast children as a social problem. The author then counters the pathologising of children through emphasis on the social problems facing them. Cosaro suggests that there is great anxiety about child victimisation in industrialised societies. On the other hand, poor children and youths in both industrialised and developing countries are blamed for their own vulnerability. The global problems affecting children include poverty, family instability and violence and Cosaro formulates proposals to address them. He gives importance to researchers adopting a stance of clear political advocacy on behalf of children.

Chapter Four is of particular interest to scholars involved in research on African childhood. This chapter provides a comparative analysis of how economic, social and cultural changes have affected families and children in both industrialised and developing societies. Cosaro states that studies on developing societies challenge Western assumptions about the nature of child-parent and sibling relations. Care is often the concern of a collective community. Given the degree of poverty in many developing countries, there is tension between education and work for children. For many children in the latter societies, there is a greater degree of separation from adults and increased dependency on one another. Complex peer cultures are prevalent and they play an important role in the lives of children.

Freidl, E., 1997, *Children of Deb Koh: Young life in an Iranian Village*, Syracuse, New York, Syracuse University Press, 306 pp., including Appendix and Glossary. ISBN: 9-780815-627579.

Friedl's anthropological study of children in the Iranian Village of Deb Koh, presents the outwardly limiting circumstances of children's lives in post-revolutionary Iran and then highlights children's strategies to surmount authority and personal demands through pastimes and games. The gendered patterns of interaction between boys and girls provide unexpected choices for movement and thought. Children are portrayed as realists making the most of meagre resources. The text is an interwoven mix with descriptions of local practices, symbolic systems, cognitive categories, stories describing adults and children's notions of conception, growing and childhood, their understanding of religion and their use of kinship terminology. The data were collected during field trips to Iran in 1989, 1992 and 1994. The book avoids obsessive situation of the author in the written text and thus concentrates the reader's attention on stories of childhood and children. Descriptive fragments and stories are juxtaposed without linking them through analysis. Readers are given the task of assessing the weight of different cultural codes as they repeat themselves through the text. Although the book is written in the ethnographic present, Friedl claims she avoids the pitfalls of this mode of writing as the processes she describes "transcend a specific time horizon" (p.xx). Because of political difficulties in Iran the author has avoided situating children too closely in identifiable families and she indeed avoids describing particular children in detail. She has attempted to maintain the anonymity of children through the use of pseudonyms. Her work lacks focus on individual children, for it tends to describe generalised patterns in the treatment of children, in adult notions of growing children and of children's ideas concerning the gendered places and spaces that boys and girls occupy. The book is therefore not successful in my view. Although the book purportedly deals with an innovative study, its generalisations create a resonance with early anthropological studies that sought to outline the "typical" trajectories of childhood.

Grauve, E. M. and D. J. Walsh, 1998, *Studying Children in Context: Theories, Methods and Ethics,* Thousand Oaks, London, New Delhi, Sage Publications, Including Index ISBN: 0-8039-7257-1, 270 pp.

The book is a manual suggesting issues to be considered in qualitative child research. The writers express the need for in-depth research on children through working with and observing children as opposed to relying on the accounts of caregivers and other adults. They provide a critique of generalisations about children formed from within particular disciplinary and theoretical orientations. For example, the writers refer to Piaget stating that although he studied children with extreme care, the context in which children were studied was contrived and the tasks Piaget gave them were imposed. Grauve and Walsh assert the importance of studying children carrying out their own meaningful tasks in familiar situations. It is questionable, however, whether any context in which children (or for that matter any other category of persons) are researched is uncontrived, as researchers always create a mediated context in their interaction with children.

Child research on children is often distanced, concentrating on public matters and institutional structures. The real experience of children is often ignored. The writers isolate guidelines for producing knowledge about children in context.

For instance:

- Children are situated historically and culturally.
- The social and historical location of researchers must be acknowledged in conducting child research.
- Social interaction between children should be the focus of study. The predominant explanation of "child" in Western literature as an isolated entity, focussing on the child's so-called internal faculties and abilities.
- The centrality of children in research on childhood. Often adult actions towards children and their conceptions concerning children become the focus of child studies. This practice should be avoided.

With regard to the above points, I do not agree that social interaction between children should be the predominant focus of child studies. Although I do not dispute the importance of peer interactions, the actions of adults and their triumphs and failures have consequences on the lives of children and these must be taken into consideration. Although it is imperative to work directly with children in the field of child studies, it is my view that adult actions and conceptions about childhood limit the space of childhood in differing social contexts and should therefore be considered.

Goldman, L. R., 1998, *Child's Play: Myth, Mimesis and Make-Believe*, New York, Oxford, Berg, 301 pp. Including Appendices, Bibliography and index, ISBN: 1-85973-918-0.

Goldman has written a careful ethnography of children's play among the Huli people of New Guinea. Play improvisation and creative life are increasingly recognised as important aspects of social life. The book counters the idea that children's play, imagination and invention are mere imitations of and preparations for adult life. His in-depth study shows how pretence is socially mediated and linguistically achieved. Issues of language acquisition, the use of metaphor, the relationship between language and identity, and how children make narrative sense of the world, are explored. Goldman focuses on children-structured play as opposed to play initiated by adults. The book shows how Huli children overlay their fantasy games with genres of myth making and storytelling. Children are thus involved in processes of reinventing cultural repositories as well as in acts of mimesis or mirroring. In Goldman's words, "In [the] slippage between "what was", "what is" and "what might be", children tread a linguistic pathway between simulation and mythologisation" (p.258). Included in the book is a careful literature review and critique of research on child-play. Goldman has found inventive methodological ways of "capturing" children's play, for example, through the use of radio microphones. Although Goldman juxtaposes his research on Huli children with research from industrialised countries on the same topic, he warns against premature comparisons as little in-depth research been done on how children "play in society" in post-colonial contexts. Goldman's book is worth reading on account of the sophistication of his theoretical ideas and the depth of his ethnographic data.

Henderson, P. C., 1999, Living with Fragility: Children in New Crossroads, Unpublished doctoral dissertation, University of Cape Town.

Living with Fragility traces the lives of sixteen African children between 1992 and 1995. It explores the intimate spaces of children's social relationships and charts the discontinuities in what they experienced. The eight girls and eight boys, aged between ten and sixteen years, resided in New Crossroads, Cape Town, a suburb marked by poverty, inadequate schooling and a history of violent intervention by the apartheid state and other power holders.

Henderson shows that childhood institutions are fragile, that children's social relationships are fragmented, as are their sense of self. The writer suggests that children's sense of self is subject to flux and interruption. Ethnographies of the children demonstrate their individuality. Nuanced descriptions of children and the changes in their lives over time challenge bald categorisations of, for example, the "African child", or, "youth at risk". The descriptions demonstrate the agency, dexterity and responsibilities of children in fluid circumstances and lead to a critical appraisal of predominant notions of childhood. The work also outlines processes of social and relational reconstitution to which children and caregivers had recourse.

Findings suggest that children marked the pain of the fissures of life within families, at school and on the streets of New Crossroads in various ways. They located themselves within multiple discourses that allowed for externalization of certain kinds of pain and not of others. Children and their families had recourse to repertoires of reconstitution of social relationship and the sense of self. These revolved around notions of ideal relationship, coherence, healing and the intercession of ancestors. Others depended on availability of discourses on political activism that envisaged solutions to current discontinuities. However, the cultural repertoires children and adults employed to "re-stitch" the social fabric did not constitute an end point in the healing processes. The lack of complete processes of reconstitution points to the layering of fragility in children's lives in New Crossroads.

Henderson used innovative ways to gather data. These included dramatic improvisation through which children reflected on their social worlds. Her work is one the few ethnographies that places emphasis on individual children in exploring themes about intimacy, violence, care, sexuality and selfhood.

Honwana, A., 1998, "'Okusiakala Ondalo Yokalye' - Let us Light a New Fire: Local Knowledge in the Post-war Healing and Reintegration of War-affiliated Children in Angola", *Consultancy Report*: Christian Children's Fund, Angola.

The report was designed to assist the Province-based War Trauma Training Project personnel in Angola to facilitate children's reintegration into families and communities. Research was carried out in the Angolan provinces of Uige, Malange, Moxico, Bie and Huambo between 1997 and 1998. The Christian Children's Research Team sought to explore local concepts, beliefs and practices related to healing, cleansing and social reintegration of war-affected children. Part One provides a background to the civil war in Angola and a rationale for studying the effects of war on children. Part Two outlines the philosophical and cosmological understanding of health and society. Part Three describes children's involvement in political violence in Angola and their experience of war. Part Four features the therapeutic strategies used by local people to treat children's war-related afflictions. Honwana emphasises the fact that notions of trauma are socially and culturally embedded and she is, therefore, critical of interventions in African conflicts that are exclusively influenced by Western biological notions of health and illness. She recommends a pluralistic approach combining and extending therapeutic strategies to include "traditional" and "modern" religious frameworks. The report draws on additional information from Mozambique.

Children in war have seen or have been responsible for the death of others. This is socially polluting as children in peacetime are generally not supposed to view the dead. In Angola 9,133 child soldiers under the age of fifteen were identified as combatants in both government and UNITA forces. UNITA had a deliberate policy of child recruitment. Children were forcibly incorporated into both armies but some of them volunteered because of political allegiance, ethnic alliances, peer pressure and the desire for food and loot. With the breakdown of social and economic structures, it was not surprising that children adhered to armies for their survival.

The report touches on children's violent initiation into armed forces, including rituals of incorporation that cut off children's links with family and society. Children who tried to escape were killed in front of other children and their killers were encouraged to drink the blood of children they had killed to avert being haunted by their spirits. Children were also given war names dissociated from family and friends — for example, "Strong", "Rambo" and "Invincible". Children were sometimes forced by their commanders to sing and dance all night long to prevent homesickness. The use of drugs like marijuana and the eating of bullet powder were rituals undertaken to induce fearlessness. Girls abducted into armed forces were forced into domestic work in military camps and to become "wives" to soldiers. (The researchers did not get testimonies about forced sex from girls because of the delicacy of the subject matter.) Despite the demobilisation of 5,171 child soldiers, children are still affected by the war. For example, there are approximately five million land mines scattered throughout the country. The majority of victims from the mines are civilians and children. (Although some peace negotiations between UNITA and the Government of Angola led to national elections, war broke out again when UNITA refused to acknowledge their defeat in the elections).

Local cosmological beliefs and practices reveal notions and practices common in many African countries. The importance of ancestors in promoting health, good fortune and the well-being of both individuals and communities is prevalent. Ancestors also purportedly punish their descendants by inflicting illness, death and infertility on the latter. They therefore have to be properly cared for by the living to avoid ancestral wrath. The living have to conduct their collective lives in ways acceptable to ancestors. Proper burial of the dead ensures their benign incorporation into the legitimate realm of the ancestors and thus establishes an acceptable relationship between the living and the dead. However, people killed in war, often do not receive proper burial and their spirits are consequently unsettled. Unhappy spirits of the unburied dead inflict a great deal of harm amongst family members of those who caused their death during war. The living, must therefore, appease wandering spirits in different ways. In Angola, war trauma is linked to the wrath of persons killed and denied proper burial.

Ill-health in Angola is therefore a socio-cultural phenomenon. Social imbalance is reflected in the physical body. Dominant Western psycho-therapeutic models are often seen as universal and applicable anywhere. Honwana concurs with other writers in claiming that the Western model is

23

also culturally constructed. It locates the causes of distress in the individual and may inadvertently undermine family and other efforts to provide care and support. Ritual processes in Mozambique and Angola do not emphasise talking as an attribute of cure and differ from the Western framework where the notion of the talking cure is prevalent. Honwana claims that ritual procedures in Angola and Mozambique separate the past from the future and allow people to start afresh. They are cleansing rituals for social reintegration. Rituals differ from region to region and are conducted by family members, healers, prophets from syncretic churches and by priests. The report gives a few case studies of individual cleansing rituals for children.

I conclude by raising questions about Honwana's claims of social reintegration for children through local ritual healing processes in Angola and Mozambique. Although rituals may have immediate efficacy in reintegrating some children into civilian life, their effects may not be guaranteed in the long term. In my view, healing is a continuous process. The lack of definite solution through the identified healing processes points to a painful experience that may not be readily accommodated. There is need for distinction between the differing reactions of individual children, some of whom may not respond in seamless ways to ritual processes.

Human Rights Committee of South Africa, 1999, *Children's Rights and Personal Rights*, Johannesburg, The Human Rights Committee of South Africa.

This special publication of the Human Rights Committee of South Africa provides a summary of recent changes in the law on children and personal rights. The changes are in line with the new constitution of South Africa." There is a commentary on discrepancies between the law and current practices concerning children. Sections of the report discuss issues about themes such as: "Just Administrative Action, Right of Access to Courts, Rights of Arrested, Detained and Accused Persons, Personal Rights — Right to Equality, Right to Human Dignity, Right to Life, Right to Freedom and Security of the Person, Right to Privacy, Democratic capacity building Institutions in Southern Africa".

The report deals with children in trouble with the law, child abuse, violence against children, sexual exploitation of children, the status of the girl-child and child soldiers. In addition to listing new laws upholding the best interests of the children, in line with the constitution, the report notes the following:

- There is no mechanism in government for assessing public spending on children. A Non-governmental Organisation, the Institute for Democracy in South Africa (IDASA) has attempted to do this in the Children's Budget Project (see Robinson and Biersteker 1997 in the reference list).
- Government departments do not identify children as a distinct group.
- Although judicial corporal punishment has been outlawed, a section of the Criminal Procedure Act regulates the use of force against fleeing suspects, including children. This means that force is often used against children fleeing the police. The Constitutional Court is supposed to have dealt with the use of force against children in the course of arrests, but this task has been delayed.

In theory, South African citizens are entitled to just administrative action, as formulated in the Just Administrative Action Draft Bill, passed in parliament in February 2000. For example, although parents are able to apply for disability grants for their disabled children, a number of problems violate their right to just administrative action. There is often a three-year period for processing applications, but in most cases, are not given adequate reasons as to why the State refuses to issue them the grants. Neither is there the possibility of appealing against refusals. Sometimes parents did not receive the grant even though their applications were successful. "Just Administrative Action" is lacking in other areas concerning children, such as: administrative bungles affecting Child Support Grant; refugee children have difficulties receiving temporary residence permits, children in the Welfare System (children adopted, fostered or removed from their parents) are handled in stressful and laborious ways between courts and institutions.

The Maintenance Act, which became law in 1998, allowed for the appointment of maintenance investigating officers to speed up the process of tracking fathers who refused or who had ceased paying maintenance. The report notes that it is very difficult to track ex-husbands and fathers and to ensure the payment of maintenance for children. As regards the Rights of Arrested, Detained and Accused Persons, there is no separate juvenile justice system for children. Children are tried by the ordinary criminal courts but proceedings involving accused children must be held in camera. There is concern about the increase in the number of children awaiting trial in adult prisons, and the long time they spend in prisons awaiting trial. The separation of children from adult prisoners is not guaranteed and this results in the abuse of children by older prisoners. The detention of children awaiting trial is supposed to be reviewed every fourteen days but no limit to the number of fourteen-day periods has yet been stipulated. Some children spend up to two years in prison awaiting trial. The Amendments to the Criminal Procedure Act 1996-1997, which became law in 1998, were designed to make it more difficult to get bail for serious offences. Children are not exempt from these provisions. The Human Rights Committee recommends that child cases be prioritised by the Police.

On the question of personal rights, the Child Support Grant instituted by the State is embarrassingly slow in terms of delivery. Introduced in April 1998, the grant was supposed to reach three million children below the age of seven by the year 2003. Only 36,433 children, (1.21 percent) were receiving the grant at the time the report was written (p. 38). This is a serious failure on the part of the State, considering that one out of every four children is malnourished and infant mortality is seven times higher for Black children than it is for White children. Corporal punishment was abolished in 1997. Before then, 35,000 boy-child offenders were whipped per year (p. 40). As far as personal security is concerned, even though there are laws against child abuse, sexual abuse is prevalent in South Africa. A 1996 Inter-Ministerial report on institutions housing children — such as Places of Safety, Schools of Industry and Reform Schools — revealed that a great deal of physical, sexual and emotional abuse of children takes place in these institutions through the actions of staff and other children.

In the case of Democratic Capacity building Institutions, between 1997 and 1998, the South African Human Rights Commission received fourteen complaints about children's rights despite changes in the legislation. These included children in adult cells, husbands not paying maintenance, corporal punishment in schools, child neglect, children beaten by the Police, harassment and assault of street children, denial of schooling for children in some farm schools and expulsion of schoolchildren due to racism. The National Youth Forum established in 1996 and attached to the Office of the Deputy President is supposed to devise government programmes to assist youths. It has been attacked for non-delivery, for being good at planning but unable to translate planning into action, for instance, into public works programmes for the youth.

In relation to Southern Africa, the report drew on the Graca Machel United Nations Report on Child Soldiers and noted that approximately 120,000 children are involved in armed conflicts throughout the world, including children in Angola, Congo, Algeria, Burundi, Congo-Brazzaville, Liberia, Rwanda, Sudan and Uganda. The South African Human Rights Commission recommends that the Organisation of African Unity (OAU) Convention on the Welfare of the Child be amended in the light of the large number of child soldiers on the continent. Peace agreements should take account of the plight of children in armed conflicts. Children involved in war should be reintegrated into society and given psychological and sociological care. Efforts should be made to reunite war-affected children with their families. Those responsible for the recruitment of children into armed forces should be brought to justice through the International Criminal Court.

James, A., C. Jenks and A. Prout, 1998, *Theorising Childhood*, Cambridge, Polity Press, 247pp., Including Index and Useful Reference List of Theories on Childhood, ISBN: 0-7456-1565-1.

Three well-known writers of the sociology of childhood provide an overview of new thinking on child studies. The authors consider childhood as a structural feature of society mirrored in children's everyday lives. The book deals with themes about how childhood is perceived in some societies. The themes include: childhood in social space, the temporality of childhood, play as childhood culture, working children, childhood in context as opposed to the abstract notion of a singular childhood, and the body and childhood. Suggestions are made as to how to research and theorise childhood. The book shows the centrality of childhood in contemporary debates concerning the State, welfare and morality.

The authors stress the importance of developing new methods in conducting research on children since researchers increasingly acknowledge children as subjects and not objects of research.

In the first section of the book, the authors provide a critique of conventional wisdom in matters concerning children by examining "pre-sociological" models of childhood. They go on to demarcate four sociological approaches to the study of childhood described as an exploratory typology that reveals new approaches and suggests avenues for future research. The four contemporary models of childhood are concerned with the socially constructed nature of childhood, the recognition of children's autonomy and agency in the construction of their worlds, a recognition of existing power relations between children and adults where children are relatively powerless and open to victimisation and the view that children form a component of all social structures in their capacity as a body of social actors entitled to rights. The models of childhood are termed — unforgivably in my view — "the socially constructed child", "the tribal child", "the minority child" and "the socio-structural child". It is argued that the models are related to four dichotomous themes that demarcate their theoretical differences. These are, agency-structure, universalism-particularism, local-global and continuity-change. My objections to the book are particularly directed to the naming of the models of childhood. Even if, for example, the notion of "tribal child" is being used with a sense of irony, I think its use is unconscionable, given its past association with colonial oppression and generalised forms of knowledge of people construed as an exotic other. According to the authors, the model of the "tribal child" refers to a stress placed by some researchers on the interrelationships between children as opposed to adults. "Tribal" in this instance seems to suggest the strong bonds between children. Given the outline of what is meant by the model, it seems unnecessary to use the term "tribal child" to describe the model. Although the models point to themes in contemporary child studies, the terms in which the models are described are insulting to children and perhaps to the researchers themselves.

Jenks, C., 1996, *Childhood*, London, Routledge, 146p., including Index, ISBN: 0-415-12014-4.

Chris Jenks' focusses his book mainly on Western conceptions about childhood. A succinct critique of his book is that he is preoccupied with adult conceptions of childhood in relation to visions of society and not with the study of children themselves. Children, therefore, are largely left out of his philosophical analysis. His book is useful insofar as it destabilises past and present hegemonic (Western) notions concerning childhood.

Jenks pertinently argues that despite a growing recognition of the plurality of childhood, a singular idea of childhood continues to be exported globally through the United Nations Declaration of the Rights of the Child and through the aid work of international organisations in the Third World. A narrow view of Western childhood is therefore generally upheld as the "correct" vision of childhood resulting in the judgement of varying family forms and practices of childcare in the Third World.

The author explores moulds within which childhood and children have been cast. These are predictably the idea of children as "savage", drawing similarities between the ways in which children and the colonial "other" have been thought about in Western discourse. Thinking within the latter paradigm creates an unquestioned hierarchy between child and adult and the naturalisation of differences. Whereas hierarchic assumptions concerning the relationship between colonial empires and the colonised have been thoroughly undermined, conceptions of childhood remain conservative and bound by skewed power relations. The child "is taken to display for adults their once untutored difference" (p. 6). Jenks examines the idea of the "natural child" where social and biological differences collapsed into one another. Here, biological changes are erroneously linked with changes in social status. This notion of childhood fails to recognise that particular social responsibilities take place at varying ages in different social contexts. Jenks argues that, contrary to popular conceptions, childhood is not a natural life stage but is socially constructed. He shows how the idea of the child is used in many social discourses as a marker of social cohesion. Childhood is conceived of as a state of becoming and rarely as a coherent social practice. Researchers, therefore, often miss the actual ways in which children live.

Jenks shows how even the critical tradition in sociology fails to accommodate children as agents of social change. He refers to the work of anthropologist Margaret Mead as challenging Western conceptions of childhood by showing the degree of autonomy and responsibility of children in a different social and cultural context. He therefore concurs with Jo Boyden's critique of the ethnocentric exportation and globalisation of the Western capitalist conception of childhood into developing countries. Jenks suggests that alternatives to dominant approaches in the study of childhood may be found in historical, comparative and phenomenological frameworks. The frameworks consecutively emphasise the importance of historically located childhood, differences in childhood in various cultural and social contexts and the different interpretative frameworks through which children give meaning to their experience. Children's perspectives become increasingly important in overturning theories of socialisation.

Jenks provides six guidelines for the study of childhood. Ideas about childhood are socially constructed. Cross-cultural analysis reveals a variety of childhood rather than a singular or universal conception of childhood. Children's practices and social relations are worthy of study in their own right. Children are active in constructing their lives and are not passive recipients of socialisation. Ethnography is a useful methodology for the study of childhood, for it gives children more voice. In creating a new paradigm of childhood, sociology engages in the process of restructuring childhood.

Jenks traces the historical antecedents to two myths and images of childhood within the Western framework. These myths encompass the tropes of the Apollonian and the Dionysian child. Derived from Greek mythology, Apollonian conceptions concerning the child portray childhood innocence, natural goodness and clarity of vision. Dionysian conceptions characterise children as a group that needs to be contained and moulded by adults in order to elicit acceptable forms of behaviour. Here, children are viewed as potentially dangerous, socially disruptive and morally dubious. Jenks, therefore, alludes to a common historical bipolarity in relation to adult notions about children.

Jenks examines the meaning of the idea of child abuse in contemporary industrialised societies. He argues that within a modernist framework promulgating the idea that Western societies have improved their methods of childcare, child abuse is seen as issuing from aberrant individuals and is not located within the social structure itself. The notion of "pervert" and "molester" places the responsibility for abuse outside everyday social relations. It is well known, however, that the majority of abusers are parents, step-parents, siblings and trusted relations. Jenks writes: "[We] are not seeking explanation in terms of occasional random occurrences or shadowy, hyperbolic figures of evil; rather, we are seeking the routines and the common place" (p. 91). Contrary to popular belief, the family is one of the most dangerous places for children to live. Jenks argues that child abuse is not a new phenomenon but is rather a constant feature of human social relations. Attention has been focused on child abuse in recent years because it conflicts with notions of social progress within the modernist conception of society. Whereas the feminist critique examined child abuse as an instance of patriarchal control, the child protection movement did not question the tenets of families and explained abuse as prevalent in what they termed "dysfunctional families". Issuing from their approach was the idea, based on behavioural psychology, that those who are abused grow up to become abusers. Within the child protection movement, it was thought that balanced relationships in a family would provide a child with the best environment for their development and that "dysfunctional families" could be "cured" through therapeutic interventions. Jenks writes, "The politics of the child protection movement was essentially rooted in the conservation of the existing social order and, as such, it contained no concerted analysis of power relations within that order" (p. 95).

Jenks suggests that in the post-modern world where discontinuity is more prevalent in people's lives than continuity, the idea of childhood no longer bears futuristic aspirations towards better prospects for humankind, but becomes a nostalgic repository for meditations on lost coherence. By way of critique of the latter views, children, although living in fragmented worlds, are often at pains to appeal to notions of continuity and to ideal constructions of society even within societies experiencing extreme forms of discontinuity (see, for example, Henderson, 2000). Jenks continues that, in "the West", where bonds between spouses have become fluid, the bond between parent and child is upheld as the "last bond of sociality". This is particularly the case as individuals have abandoned collective social and political goals in disillusioned retreat from belief in meta-theories concerning emancipation. Child abuse is met with a great deal of anger in public discourse because it seems that attacks on children threaten the last link of sociality.

Jenks explores the erosion of childhood or the blurring between adult and child in the contemporary context. He examines public response to the murder of two-year-old James Bulger by two boys in Britain. Bulger's murder raised questions about the nature of childhood and children's capacity for action. Childhood innocence seemed eroded through the almost inconceivable murder of a child by other children. Jenks argues that the case provides a platform for consideration of the dissonance between children's own experience of their status — being a child — and the institutional form that childhood takes. From an acknowledgement of the latter point it becomes clear that the plurality of childhood needs to be recognised not only across cultural divides but also within societies.

John, M., 1995, "Rights in a Free Market Culture", pp. 105-137, in S. Stephens' *Children and the Politics of Culture*, New Jersey, Princeton University Press, ISBN: 0-691-04329-9, including index.

Mary John argues that, although on the surface, the United Nations Convention on the Rights of the Child creates an ideal vision for the way in which children should live, it is intrinsically flawed. Children were left out of deliberations on and the drafting of the Convention and their absence in this regard reveals how the international community implicitly views them. The author suggests that the Convention does not acknowledge the power that children have in different social contexts. The Convention excludes political rights for children, which is a serious omission in the writer's view. A child is defined in terms of the Convention as someone below eighteen years of age. This grouping, however, includes people who are parents, workers, soldiers and who have responsibilities in varying social domains (p. 107).

One of the most contentious assumptions of the Convention is that children's rights are best maintained within families. The feminist critique has shown how families can be dangerous for weaker members and that they are characterised by unequal power relations that are open to abuse. The Convention assumes that adults relate to children in loving and altruistic ways and hence contains an idealisation of adult child relations. Families may be characterised by paternalistic practices, in relation to children, that restrict their autonomy in numerous ways. In contrast to conservative politicians in Britain who call for a return to family values, the Opposition locates the causes of children's problems in structural and economic factors and hence advocates the need for government programmes. In many European countries, the institutions beyond the family play a large role in the socialisation of children. Many of these institutions are characterised by what John, referring to Ingleby (1985, see reference list) calls the "Psy-Complex". The term means that many professionals aim to apply psychological technology to social problems. The result of locating social "health" in the individual is that where family socialisation is inadequate, children are thought of as potentially dangerous. Little focus is directed towards how socio-economic problems or the failure of caregivers may affect children.

The Convention has also universalised particular Western models of notions of self and of children's development into individuals. John, in agreement with Robert Coles (1986, see Fiona Ross' annotated bibliography), suggests that "assumptions about child rearing mediate with political regimes" (p. 107). Drawing on anthropological evidence, John shows how the boundaries of the self and the non-self vary in different socio-cultural contexts. The notion of child and maturation promulgated by the Convention emphasises an end point of a high degree of personal control and the idea that mature persons are governed internally as opposed to externally. In many contexts in the world, power is seen to be located in a field of social and spiritual forces, which include the individual but go beyond the said contexts. The role of peer groups in the socialisation of the individual tends to be ignored within the Western framework.

John argues that conservative policies, for example, government cuts in financial aid to schools, result in schools marketing themselves. Lists of child excellence for marketing purposes promote a narrow form of individualism that cannot accommodate children who are not as gifted as others. New social policies in Britain emphasise community care. However, one of the consequences of shrinking the welfare State is that women and children increasingly take on the burden of looking after the young, the sick and the aged. The burden on children's shoulders increases with the insistence on increased responsibility within communities (p. 134).

Levine, S., 1999, "Bittersweet Harvest: Children's Work and the Global March Against Child Labour in the Port-apartheid State, in *Critique of Anthropology*, vol. 19(2): 139-155.

The article explores recent transformations in child labour legislation in a context of rapid democratic change in South Africa. Susan Levine stresses the agency of children working in the vine lands of the Western Cape Province. She outlines children's insistence on the right to work and the complexities that emerge when local conceptions about child autonomy meet global demands for child labour. Recent anti-child labour campaigns in South Africa fail to provide economic support for poor black and coloured children who work to sustain families and households. The author argues that international legislation against child labour ignores the role of children in a globally flexible labour market. By separating child from adult exploitation, international discourses perpetuate the conditions that give rise to child labour. Levine makes recommendations about controlling the conditions of child work in the wine industry in South Africa. The article is a summarised version of her doctoral thesis at Temple University of Philadelphia entitled, "In the Shadow of the Vine: Child Labor in South Africa".

Machel, G., 1996, *Impact of Armed Conflict on Children: Report of the Expert of the Secretary-General, Ms. Graca Machel, submitted pursuant to General Assembly Resolution 48/157*, Geneva, United Nations, 72 pp. No ISBN number.

The report developed out of a number of regional consultations covering different parts of the world, and out of field trips the writer made to Angola, Cambodia, Colombia, Northern Ireland, Lebanon and Rwanda. Graca Machel introduces the report describing the widespread involvement of children in armed conflict. She suggests that a preponderance of child soldiers is indicative of a global moral vacuum where the "sacred and protected spaces" of childhood have been eroded. She notes that, in 1995, there were 30 on-going wars within states. In a post-colonial global context, the predominance of wars within states denotes competition over resources under conditions of increasing poverty and economic failure. Machel suggests that children should have no part in warfare. Her assumption is that children are a unifying force bringing people together on ethical grounds across ideological and cultural divides.

One characteristic of contemporary wars is that the distinction between civilians and combatants disappears. Civilians form ninety percent of war victims (p.14). Machel notes large-scale human rights violations against women and children and the dispersal and uprooting of many people. It is argued that children are more easily incorporated directly into armed combat because of the development of lighter weapons. Children also play supporting roles in war, for example, as cooks, spies, porters and messengers. The report notes that children are recruited in various ways: some are forced into service, others volunteer, and some are conscripted. In countries with weak administrative systems, conscription is not done systematically from a register. Recruits may be seized arbitrarily from schools, orphanages and streets. Wealthy families can often avoid the seizure of their children, but the same cannot be said for poorer families. Recruitment of younger children seems to increase when educational facilities for children collapse. Children may join for their own protection, for ideological reasons and to gain access to a tangible form of power.

Once recruited as soldiers, children are often subjected to brutal initiation ceremonies. They are involved in support functions but also in armed combat. Although the majority of child soldiers are boys, girls are also recruited. In addition to carrying out other tasks, girls are often forced into sexual relationships with male soldiers. Children are sometimes perpetrators and witnesses to atrocities.

The report proposes that children under the age of eighteen should be removed from armed forces. It is noted that, to date, no peace treaty has formally recognised child combatants. Processes of social reintegration are recommended for former child soldiers. Reintegration programmes could assist in re-establishing contact between children and their families, and in ensuring that former child soldiers have access to continuing education. Machel notes the particular difficulty of the social reintegration for girls who have been sexually abused. Cultural beliefs often deny space for girls to acknowledge their experience. Public knowledge of their having been sexually abused may mitigate against marriage in some social contexts.

The report makes suggestions for the prevention of future recruitment of child soldiers. It contains a section on the dispersal of children in war and suggests strategies for repatriating children as well as specific recommendations concerning displaced children.

The report contains a section on sexual exploitation and gender-based violence in war. Most child victims of sexual abuse are girls but Machel notes that young boys are also sometimes victims of rape and that instances of sexual abuse involving boys is under-reported. Rape is a form of torture that compounds a multifaceted disruption of social boundaries in war. Machel notes that "the failure to denounce and prosecute wartime rape is partly the result of its mischaracterisation as an assault against honour or a personal attack rather than a crime against the physical integrity of the victim" (p.32). Twelve case studies of gender-based violence carried out for the report pointed out members of the armed forces as the main perpetrators of sexual violence in times of war. The report makes recommendations for the curtailment of gender-based violence in war.

The report features a section on land-mines and their effects on civilian populations, including children. It is noted that populations in at least 68 countries where 110 million land-mines are reportedly buried (p. 34) are often casualties of explosions. In Angola, 8,000 children are amputees due to land-mine explosions (p. 34). Machel concludes: "African children live on the continent most plagued by land-mines — there are as many as 37 million mines in at least 19 African countries" (p. 34). The report calls for mine clearance and the rehabilitation of victims. It also calls for a ban on the use of land-mines in international law.

Machel examines the impact of sanctions on children, explores issues of child health in times of war, and suggests ways of promoting psychological recovery and social reintegration of children in the aftermath of armed conflict. The writer notes the limitations of Western models of therapeutic care and suggests the use of culturally sensitive methods of cleansing and healing.

Finally, Machel outlines inadequacies in existing humanitarian legislation on children and war. Issues concerning reconciliation in the aftermath of war, and conflict resolution, are explored. Global organisations playing a role in mediating the effects of armed conflict and involved in child care are listed together with recommendations for their future activities.

Myers, W., 1999, "Considering Child Labour: Changing Terms. Issues and Actors at the International Level", pp.13-26, in *Childhood: A Global Journal of Child Research*, Vol. 6 (1).

William Myers notes the broadening dimension of debate on child labour issues at an international level. The variety of child work situations and their differing effects on children have been acknowledged and more attention is being given to children's views about work. Erstwhile action against child labour has been discredited as ineffective.

For more than a century, there has been the idea that children should not work even if they wanted or needed to work. Myers takes an unusual stance suggesting that the latter idea can at one level be linked to a desire to protect adult access to the job market. He mentions, for example, that within the tenets of trade unionism and in many social policies, it is argued that the best interests of children are served by ensuring the full employment of parents with living wages that enable them to fulfil their responsibilities towards their children.

Children should not be viewed in isolation when assessing their involvement in work as they have links with families and within communities that describe the social context of their work as well as their identities. Myers argues that child labour should not be narrowly viewed as a violation of labour law, as interruption of children's education or as an expression of poverty. The contemporary emphasis is not so much on reducing child employment but on lobbying against harmful working situations.

Working children at two international conferences in India and The Netherlands complained that global policies established for their protection are often detrimental to children (p. 15). In situations where children's work contributes substantially to their survival and to that of their family members, policies that result in the suppression of particular forms of work have made children even poorer in the long run and have sometimes forced them into more invisible and more arduous ways of working.

New research findings describe a broad diversity of children's work. In line with the work of Jo Boyden *et al.* (1996, see bibliography). Myers argues that similar kinds of work and similar policy interventions do not have the same effect in different social and cultural contexts. Consequently, there is tension between the need for local understanding of the context of children's work and the international movement towards generalised "remedies", global standards and rights.

Myers' article refers to two ways in which information about children and work has been gathered. The first draws on information from large-scale surveys such as the World Bank's Living Standards Measurement Surveys. The second draws on detailed studies of children and their work. Myers refers to several comparative studies where survey information has been studied to extract data about working children. He shows how detailed studies of children's work in particular localities are rare and have been undertaken mainly by anthropologists.

Most of the current policies on children are based on outdated ideas about the psychosocial development of children. Development specialists have often ignored the fact that many of the world's children work. Myers writes:

> the popular notion that all children develop through the same universal set of biologically determined stages to some sort of end-point considered as "maturity" — the conceptual framework now underlying several international child protection activities — has given way, among specialists, to a more social view of human development that emphasises the formative importance of children's transaction with their social environment (p. 21).

Myers suggests two ways in which child labour has been defined. Trade unions, consumer groups and the International Labour Organisation seem to adhere to the idea that child labour is work undertaken by children of an economic nature. Their claim is that children should not engage in any economic activity at all. A second definition of child labour suggests that it is work undertaken by children that is injurious to their well-being. Here, there is an attempt to separate detrimental working conditions from work itself. UNICEF and the International Working Group on Child Labour have adopted the idea of assessing child work in terms of a continuum where one pole denotes work that is intolerably harmful and where the other pole denotes work that is completely beneficial. Positive and negative aspects of child work should be evaluated separately and then balanced against one another.

Myers concludes that there are no real solutions without the full participation of children and their families. He notes, however, that this is a minority position and that large organisations such as ILO tend to concentrate on demarcating the most dangerous working conditions experienced by children.

Nieuwenhys, O., 1996, "The Paradox of Child Labour and Anthropology". *Annual Review of Anthropology*, 25:237-51, ISSN: 0084-6570.

Olga Nieuwenhys' article provides an excellent critique and overview of ideas concerning child labour as promulgated until recently by international organisations. As can be seen in referring to other more recent works included in the annotated bibliography, child labour organisations are beginning to accommodate some of her criticisms. Nieuwenhys states that, within a Western framework, childhood is dissociated from the performance of valued work and that the school is purportedly the only legitimate institutional space for children outside the family. Children's agency in the creation and negotiation of value is, therefore, denied. Nieuwenhys argues against ideas promulgated globally by organisations such as the International Labour Organisation (ILO) where paid factory work has come to define work regarded as harmful to children and where unpaid work in homes and within family undertakings remains unquestioned. Underpinning the moral condemnation of child labour is the idea that children's role in modern society is ideally one of dependency and passivity. Nieuwenhys examines the historical reasons for the phasing out of child labour in the 19th Century industrial Britain. Industrialists did not want the competition from cheap child labour in their determination to mechanise production processes. A distinction arose between illegitimate child work, defined as work in factories, and other forms of work considered suitable. The suitable work contained socialising and training aspects and included housekeeping, child-minding, farm work, errands, domestic work, etc. Nieuwenhys writes that the distinction between harmful and suitable work, as defined by Western legislation, has provided a framework for most contemporary governmental and bureaucratic approaches to child work with far-reaching consequences. Because of the latter distinction, ILO, for example, inadvertently sanctioned unpaid work for children in homes regardless of the implications for the child. International discourse on child labour ignores social meanings attached to local systems of age ranking and universalises a Western conception of life stages and biological maturity. Because of this, the early introduction of children to artisanal occupations, for example — which may be crucial to the child's socialisation within a particular context — is blocked.

ILO denies children the right to work for their own upkeep. Nieuwenhys pertinently writes that, "The denial of gainful employment is all the more paradoxical since family and State often fail to provide children with what they need to lead a normal life" (p. 240).

In colonial settings, Nieuwenhys points out that anthropologists romanticised child work as socialisation and as being well adapted to economic and social levels of pre-industrial society. In line with the theme of romanticisation, later studies argued that large families in Africa and other parts of the Third World acted as safety nets for their members. Family-budget studies in the 1970s suggested that children contributed to their own subsistence in peasant economies. The studies failed to particularise historical, cultural and social roles of children in these contexts. It has been recognised in recent feminist studies that the household is not an unproblematic unit and that it is characterised by hierarchies in terms of gender and age.

National and international organisations such as UNICEF, World Health Organisation, ILO and international charities including the International Catholic Bureau, Save the Children, Defence of Children International and Anti-Slavery International have until recently harboured the neo-classical belief that child labour is a problem of household economics. Nieuwenhys argues that a typical feature of the publications produced by the above organisations is a moral preoccupation with the abolition of child labour through legislation and "a zealous belief in the desirability of extending Western childhood ideals to poor families worldwide". This leads to the criminalisation of the ways in which many poor people survive and poor children are brought up — an irony when modern economies increasingly decrease their capacities to protect poor children through neo-liberal trade policies (p. 242).

Nieuwenhys counters the persistent idea that school is an antidote to child work.

She concludes that hierarchies of age, gender and kinship combine to define mandatory work for children and sometimes condemn paid work. She writes:

> By legitimising children's obligation to contribute to survival and denying them the right to seek personal gain, these hierarchies effectively constrain them to a position of inferiority within the family. It is not so much their factory employment as their engagement in low-productivity and domestic tasks that defines the ubiquitous ways poor children are exploited in today's developing world (p. 245).

Because of a global institutional failure to support children, the legitimacy of barring children from remunerative employment becomes questionable. Children who are in paid employment encounter age and gender hierarchies that often confine their work in undervalued domestic domains. Nieuwenhys suggests that areas of future research could encompass the clash between neo-liberal economies and the global ideology of childhood. Researchers could also examine children's agency in seeking paid work, creating value and invading constraining structures based on seniority.

Ndebele, N., 1995, "Recovering Childhood: Children in South African National Reconstruction", pp. 321-333, in S. Stephens' *Children and the Politics of Culture*, New Jersey, Princeton University Press, ISBN: 0-691-04329-9, including Index.

Njabulo Ndebele, the well-known South African writer and academic, follows themes on the mistreatment of children in South African literature. One theme he discards is the idea that a difficult childhood is sometimes regarded as a rite of passage through which both greatness and individual character flaws may emerge. Ndebele refers to Thomas Mofolo's book, *Chaka: King of the Zulus* in which Chaka's difficult childhood is linked with his future greatness and his propensity for cruelty. Ndebele suggests that "images of the travails of children are powerful metaphors of indictment, calling for the urgent redemption of society" (p. 322). Images of child death imply an ultimate degradation of society. Ndebele notes child death during the 1976 student uprising in South Africa and the increasing incorporation of the young into leadership positions in grassroots organisations against the State. Violence against children as a metaphor for social disease and fragmentation loses its shock effect when children are killed by both State and people in conflict within communities. Ndebele states that the narrative forms in which violence has been reported in South Africa limit understanding through, among other things, distancing effects and the listing of political organisations as entities responsible for deaths. Ndebele suggests that the protection of childhood by adults contains healing for adults. He writes: "[I]n nurturing |childhood| we confirm the need for culture, recreation and creativity" (p. 331). Ndebele therefore links childhood redemption to the reconstruction of society.

Nordstrom, C., 1997, *A Different Kind of War Story*, Philadelphia, University of
    Pennsylvania Press, 254 pp. including Index, ISBN: 19104-6097.

Carolyn Nordstrom's book is an account of the civil war in Mozambique.
She suggests that violence cannot be defined in a limiting sense by focusing
on its overt forms such as mutilation, rape and death. Violence to personhood,
to the social location of individuals, to relationships with ancestors and with
parents, spouses and siblings expands researchers' conception of violence.
The author tells stories often through Mozambicans' experiences in the
fifteen-year war, showing how many survived creatively despite brutality
and terror.

Although the book does not concentrate predominantly on children, its
themes create some parameters in which understanding children's experience
of war could be broadened beyond notions of passive victimhood. She
suggests the importance of listening to stories of experience and to
accepting areas of children's silence. Nordstrom touches on the abduction
of children into RENAMO forces. She discusses children being accommodated
by civilians after having witnessed the deaths of their parents and their own
families (pp. 52-53). She relates a number of children's songs on pages
138-141, and argues that children are creators in their own right. Following
the work of the important anthropologist, Veena Das, Nordstrom makes the
point that children are often treated as if they have no philosophies or
feelings about war. The children's songs contain their commentaries on
displacement, missing home, bravado in the face of danger, the wish to
protect themselves, their parents and their communities, the feelings of
orphans, and a determination to survive. One song demonstrating a street-
wise toughness proclaimed, "They got my mother, they got my father but
they won't get me" (p. 141).

Nordstrom refers to the creativity of healers in forming rituals to "take
the war out" of abductees and soldiers, including children. She claims that
rituals were compassionate, embodied and supportive and strove to re-link
individuals with community.

Children and adults created systems of knowledge and survival. For
example, orphaned street children in Zambesi Province often had the most
current information on attacks, troop movements, zones of safety and
danger and resources. They created organisations on the street to care for
younger orphans. Many were anxious to go to school and they gathered
information about which schools would accept them. How to get resources
to attend school was a frequent topic of conversation.

Nordstrom concludes that although people created remarkable systems of recovery and justice, little support could be gained from powerful socio-political institutions.

Although Nordstrom's book contains a good theoretical overview of literature on violence and war, it lacks in-depth, systematically collected data from Mozambique itself.

Omari, C. K. and D. A. S. Mbilingi, 1997, *African Values and Child Rights: Some Cases from Tanzania,* Dar Es Salaam: Dar Es Salaam University Press, 67 pp. ISBN: 9976-60-30-2.

This book is a generalised account of the ways in which adults view children and children's rights in Tanzania. Omari and Mbilingi drew on "30 ethnic groups" to support their findings. No attempt has been made to accommodate change within contemporary African contexts and to chart the effects of change on institutions. Neither do the authors show any contestation of values between different interest groups, for example, in terms of gender.

The Introduction distinguishes childhood from adulthood in African societies in a timeless and ahistorical way. Processes of initiation mark the passage from childhood to adulthood for both boys and girls. The ability to produce children is a marker of adulthood although most women are relegated to the status of perpetual minors. In the writers' view, adulthood is linked to authority and decision-making. Also noted is the predominance of joking relations between alternate generations that contributed to the protection of children by their grandparents.

The authors criticise the United Nations Convention on the Rights of the Child because of a Western bias in defining a child as someone under eighteen years and its assumption of the pertinence of individual rights. In Tanzania, the writers argue that a child is part of a community and cannot be separated from it. Omari and Mbilingi suggest that there is a problem in separating individual rights from children's expected roles within communities. Similarly, there is a difficulty in distinguishing child labour and tasks undertaken as part of a child's training process for effective adulthood. Individual rights are therefore embodied in group rights. The writers state that individual rights are difficult to uphold in social contexts of civil war, ethnic and class privilege.

Chapter Two examines the relationship between mothers and children, suggesting that if a woman's rights improve so do those of her children. Children are placed within particular family structures in both matrilineal and patrilineal groupings. Children are introduced to various kinds of work according to gender and age. Women and children are reportedly protected in times of war. The authors must surely be referring to a utopian past, for children and women are certainly participants and victims in armed conflict, as borne out in contemporary wars in Africa.

In terms of the rights of a child, the writers claim that, in Africa, children have the right to a name and family and that children born out of wedlock, as well as orphans, are incorporated into families. Having been granted a place within family structures, children are afforded rituals of protection. The authors suggest forms of shelter, food distribution, circumcision and education for children — all within an idealised framework of "tradition". The book lacks detailed descriptions of contemporary childhood in Tanzania and for the most part it offers a model of childhood that may in many respects differ widely from the ways in which children live. A final chapter entitled "Changing African Values and the UN Convention" deals with issues concerning children's education and child labour. The low enrolment of girls in schools, as compared with boys, is noted, and so is child work beyond the household. Children contribute to family survival by working on tea, sisal and tobacco plantations. They are also involved in mining and informal business.

No details are provided about migration, urbanisation and the characteristics of urban or rural poverty in helping to chart changes within family structures and the ways in which children live.

Reynolds, P., 1995, "Youth and Politics in South Africa", pp. 218-240, in S. Stephens (ed.) *Children and the Politics of Culture*, New Jersey, Princeton University Press, 366 pp., including Index, ISBN: 0-691-04329-9.

The 1976 protest by African school children against Afrikaans as a medium of instruction in schools produced a generation of politicised and politically active youth. The children's struggle extended to include broader political change. Reynolds notes that a partial state of emergency declared in July 1985 led to large-scale detentions that affected many children for the first time. By November 1996, there were approximately 4,000 children in detention. (Cf. Thomas A., 1990, "Violence and Child Detainees", in B. McKendrick and W. Hoffman,(eds.) *People and Violence in South Africa*, Cape Town, Oxford University Press).

The paper charts young people's experiences of apartheid during the 1980s and early 1990s. The study began in 1991 with seven students at the University of Cape Town. Together with Reynolds, they explored the social means of support on which they relied to survive their involvement in political activities aimed against the Apartheid State. The group had experienced a total of 30 years of imprisonment between them. All but one person had experienced torture and solitary confinement. Some of them had gone into exile for short periods. The seven young people expanded the study to include 25 people with whom they were connected.

The paper encompasses three major themes: tracing the continuities and changes in the political culture of youths as agents of change; youths' struggle for legitimate representation, and the negotiation of young people's identity within the family and within communities. Reynolds writes: "The politics of culture has to do with the process of accepting, selecting, inventing, re-ordering and mastering. Form is expressed in the present in terms of high politics and of private life" (p. 223).

In telling the stories of their lives, the students traced continuity in political consciousness between and across generations. Reynolds writes carefully about individual students and their stories. For example, one student had a mother who was politically active in the 60s. Another young man was inspired as a child by a newspaper vendor who told him about the events of the day. Yet another was sent by his parents to live with an uncle who turned out to be a leading political figure. All the students said they had become politically active at school and in the university. None of them became politically involved at the request of guardians. They were gradually incorporated into political activities ranging from street protests through the experience of torture and clandestine alliance to banned organisations.

Reynolds points out that the duration of the youth rebellion spanned fifteen years and that this is a long time to sustain resistance in the face of a harsh regime. She names five sources of endurance and social support on which the student's drew. These are students' own individuality, their families, their peer groups, political comrades and prisoner solidarity.

Reynolds concludes that it is important to listen to the stories of the young who bore the brunt of years of revolution. If their stories are not told, people "will not know how they have enriched the future" (p. 237). Reynolds' approach is important, for it insists on the retention of moral and socially concerned attitudes among young people who contributed to political transformation. This is in stark contrast to commentators describing young people who came through the struggle as "the lost generation" and as "youth at risk". Implicit within the latter ideas is the notion that youths who participated in violent activities in situations of social conflict would automatically perpetuate violence in new forms in times of peace. Reynolds is at pains to demonstrate the strength and discipline of many youths who contributed, as children, to social transformation in ways "that may have been greater than the sum of their numbers" (p. 238).

Reynolds, P., 1996, *Traditional Healers and Childhood in Zimbabwe*, Athens, OH: Ohio University Press, pp. 183, including Appendix, ISBN: 0-8214-1122-5.

The book provides an understanding of children's place in cosmology. It explores how conceptions about childhood influence healers' treatment of children and the acquisition of knowledge about healing across generations. Reynolds conducted her study between 1982 and 1983 in Mashonaland, Zimbabwe. The work involved 60 healers in three areas spanning town and country in the aftermath of the Zimbabwean war. There are six "generative metaphors" around which Reynolds explores notions of childhood and acquisition of knowledge by children through their relationship with healers. These are:

- Tracing healers' conceptions about childhood that influence their practice and moral discourse.
- Tracking the transmission of knowledge between *nanga* (healers) and the young.
- Undertaking social analysis of children as healer's assistants in order to reflect on identity, possession and dreams, and the relationship between individuals, spirituality and community.
- Charting what healers and children learn about flora and fauna. Here, Reynolds explores the assumption that healers draw on a body of knowledge accumulated in childhood while working and living with healers. This is an age-old practice, despite healers' claims that knowledge is not transferred across generations but individually acquired through direct communication with ancestors.
- Exploring war and trauma for children and uncovering the flexibility of ritual in addressing children's pain.
- Considering the question of evil, a theme seldom dealt with in literature on healing and childhood.

The aim of the work is to encourage research on children in Africa as patients or clients and as healers under training. There is a lacuna in the literature on medical anthropology connected with these issues. Very little has been written on the spiritual interpretation of children's ailments and their cure.

Reynolds explores self-knowledge and self-creation through healers recollection of dreams in their childhood that presaged their calling as healers. Dreams may be described as "techniques of self" (Michel Foucault 1984:369, cited in Reynolds 1996:25). Healers refer to themselves as "pockets of the shades". They are conduits in a process of communication between ancestors and their descendants. When children dream, they select episodes to relate to adults. Some children's dreams are dismissed but some are seen as messages from ancestors. In fact, ancestors who send dreams to a child may be appealing for a debt to be paid, a spirit may be calling for compensation to be made to a family for his death in war, a shade may communicate that the child is being selected as a future healer. Dreams are seriously considered in times of illness and misfortune. Children are active partners in healing processes in that they can use dreams as part of the conversation between themselves and healers.

Healers identified three causes that had disturbed children during the war. Children who witnessed death were sometimes plagued by the spirit of the dead. They might relive visions of the war. A child could become ill because an unsettled spirit sought revenge for a wrongful death. The family would have to compensate the family of the dead person in order for the child to recover. Children who had power over others during the war had to be returned to the bottom of hierarchies defined by family, community and school. This was done without judgement in purification rituals and through on-going contact and attentive care.

Reynolds explored Zezuru conceptions about evil through a reflection on notions of childhood. The transition from childhood to adulthood in Zezuru culture is a "transition from innocence to social identity and self-integrity. Evildoers are adults who failed to achieve that transition according to the norms and ethics of community" (p. 95). Reynolds further asserts that victims of evil are often innocent children or weak adults. Healing therefore strengthens the social identity of individuals and of communities.

Reynolds worked with two groups of children, one where children lived with healers, and one where they did not. She sought to test their knowledge of plants. It was found that most children from both groups had knowledge of plants and medicine. The depth of knowledge could not be ascertained. Reynolds showed how the religious life of communities constituted an area of integration for children. They gained knowledge by assisting with consultations and by gathering herbs. She suggested that the nature of knowledge was common but that its practice was specialised.

Reynolds' work is an example of a careful ethnography of African children relying on contextualised knowledge and observation, the kind of work that is all too rare in the study of childhood.

Richards, P., 1996, *Fighting for the Rain Forest: War, Youth and Resources in Sierra Leone*, London, James Curry and Heinemann, 182 pp., including Index, ISBN: 0-435-07406-7.

Yusuf Bangura and Ibrahim Abdullah (1997) provide incisive criticisms of Paul Richards' book on youth and war in Sierra Leone. Their views are given above in the annotated bibliography but are briefly reiterated here. The above writers claim that Richards' book is thin on ethnography and is also factually incorrect.

Richards argues that global explanations concerning contemporary small wars are inadequate and need more fine-grained analysis. Current explanations for wars in Africa, for example, encompass the idea of a "new barbarism" (propounded by American journalist Robert Kaplan in 1993). Here, Africa is imagined as a wild and dangerous place where violence is driven by environmental and cultural imperatives in which the West has no part. Richards is at pains to challenge the "new barbarism" thesis. Kaplan's explanation of the war in Sierra Leone was that it was due to population pressure, environmental collapse and the fact that government troops had little control of the forested eastern and southern areas of the country. Poverty in the cities as well as land hunger and drought in rural areas contributed, according to Kaplan, to the actions of criminally inclined migrants, who had a propensity for violence and little political purpose. Captured within the idea of "new barbarism" was, therefore, the notion of random irrational terror.

Richards argues that what appeared to be anarchic violence was rational and effective, and that the techniques of terror employed by forest fighters compensated for lack of equipment. Terror was used to achieve strategic outcomes. Richards suggests that forest rebels used cultural resources concerning knowledge of the forest in practical and symbolic ways. They had an awareness of modern media and the propaganda opportunities they provide. They compelled media coverage of their explanations for the war through the use of terror. Being marginalised, they had no other means of attracting media attention. Richards attempts to locate the Sierra Leonean war in the context of global hybrid relations in which America and Europe played a violent part.

The work is described as an ethnographic study drawing on a framework comprising of theoretical approaches concerning practice, performance, discourse and cultural theory. The book contains eight chapters. Chapter One is an account of the conflict started by the Revolutionary United Front (RUF). Chapter Two analyses the political economy of State recession in Sierra Leone and its impact on the youth. Chapter Three accounts for how rebels in the forest on the Liberian border built a movement by capturing young people. It also examines 500 years of forest intervention in which outside interests played a part. Chapter Four outlines three local texts linking forest resources and violence. The first is a young combatant's experience of fighting. The second is based on a Mende oral history from the Gola Forest commenting on the violent exploitation of forest resources in the last days of the Slave Trade in the mid-19th Century. The third tracks the stories of two young diamond miners making a living in the diamond camps of the border region by showing war films on a portable rig. Here, films like "Rambo" come to take on a local meaning and give local wars a symbolic link with ideas from elsewhere. Chapter Five expands on the relationship young people have with international media and how ideas within the media take on local meanings where a local position in relation to global social change is imagined and shaped. Chapter Six challenges the idea that the war was driven by an environmental crisis. It is suggested that deforestation has a long history in Sierra Leone and that the social and technical inventiveness employed over the centuries in response to changes within the forest are not at an end. Richards insists that the war was launched because of political failures on the part of the State. Chapter Seven shows how rebels introduced schools into their areas and how this was in contradistinction to the official State that failed to provide children with consistent and meaningful education. Chapter Eight argues that youths in Sierra Leone are committed to political modernity and that they desire transparent and accountable State institutions and civil society. An Afterword tracks negotiations between RUF and the government in subsequent years as well as the national elections that brought an end to the war.

Scheper-Hughes, N. & S. Sargent (eds.), 1998, *Small Wars: The Cultural Politics of Childhood*, Berkeley, Los Angeles, London, University of California Press, 429 pp. including Index, ISBN: 0-520-20918-4.

Nancy Scheper-Hughes and Carolyn Sargent note in the introduction to their book the "marginal social, economic, and legal status of the world's children". They suggest that childhood is "a story of resilience and survival against odds" (p. 1). The book contains a series of articles that demonstrate childhood as a public concern as well as the failure of private families and households to care for children and protect them from global political and economic interventions. The authors argue that children cannot be set apart from the cultural politics of everyday life. Some chapters chart the detrimental effects of global economic policies on the health of children, policies issuing from the International Monetary Fund (IMF) and its structural adjustment policies. Several chapters demonstrate how new reproductive technologies have changed ways in which people think about conception, abortion and biological and social parenting. The book examines the reproduction of children in social contexts that belie idealised notions of childhood. The structural violence of worlds inhabited by the majority of the world's children provides a focus for the studies. Discourses on child abuse, which often underplay the social aspects of child oppression, are placed in perspective.

The first section of the book entitled "Negotiating Parenthood and Childhood" contains a number of essays dealing with the impact of contemporary biomedical reproductive technologies and their effects on cultural and political notions of kinship, personhood and parenthood. Lyn Morgan examines local village notions concerning the unborn child in Ecuador. She describes the status of the unborn child as indeterminate and as being sometimes dangerous. A foetus is seen as belonging to a group of spirit-beings, and a baby only becomes a person after baptism. Cultural notions concerning the status of the unborn are coupled with considerable tolerance towards traditional forms of abortion. The author suggests that with the introduction of biomedical interventions such as ultra-sound, and a spread of North American Protestant fundamentalism, notions about the foetus might change. Foetuses might be given the status of persons with rights, a development that could link with anti-abortion lobbies. Mary Picone traces the history of infanticide in Japan and explores rituals to appease the spirits of aborted children who are thought to have the capacity to inflict misfortune on the living. Daphna Birenbaum-Carmeli and Elizabeth Roberts look at conflicts between genetic and social parenting in the light of new reproductive technologies. John Brett and Susan Niermeyer examine the tendency to over-diagnose jaundice in young children, a condition that often corrects itself. The authors claim that biomedical interventions need to be examined in terms of their social implications, one of them being that bonding between mothers and newborn children is interrupted. Mathew

Gutmann explores the tensions of gender inversions in working-class areas of Mexico City where fathers increasingly have to look after children while mothers work. Fathers and children refer to a local illness described as *mamitis*: frustrated longing for the absent mother. Appeals to *mamitis* put pressure on mothers to return home where they "belong". In a study conducted in Israel, Meira Weiss examines the response of parents to their disfigured children and shows that most parents try to abandon or to segregate such children. The article raises questions about unconditional love and the ethics of parenthood.

In Part Two of the book, "The Cultural Politics of Child Survival", Caroline Brettell links child abandonment with economic crisis in Portugal. Linda Whiteford (in the Dominican Republic and Cuba) and Carolyn Sargent and Michael Harris (in Jamaica) link IMF structural adjustment policies to the shrinking of national health systems and a general deterioration of women's health and that of children. Child abandonment in the above articles is linked to the economic pressure on young mothers having children out of wedlock. In times of economic crisis, single mothers may place their children in orphanages while hoping to reunite with them at a later stage. Sargent and Harris note a propensity to abandon male children more readily in Jamaica. Within an ideological gender framework, boys are considered potentially destructive in female-headed households. In a study of populations in the Northern Cape of South Africa, Leonard Lerer seeks to de-medicalise malnutrition by using the word "hunger". He examines a local explanation for the "the Rogue", an illness caused by hunger. The Rogue refers to children who succumb easily to malnutrition. It is linked, in the eyes of mothers, with absent fathers whose abandonment of their children becomes manifest in the wasted condition of their children.

Part Three: "Small Wars, Children and Violence" contains essays on harm inflicted on children. Jill Korbin writes about mothers who killed their children. J.S. Fontaine writes on ritual and satanic abuse of children in England. Nancy Scheper-Hughes deals with sex abuse of children in the Catholic Church in Ireland. Maria Olujic concentrates on Croatian children in the aftermath of the Bosnian war. Phillipe Bourgeois focuses on drug and gun use in the inner-city areas of America. Finally, Nancy Scheper-Hughes and Daniel Hoffman write about Brazilian street children and their occupation of urban space while Donna Goldstein dwells on child discipline and punishment in a Brazilian shantytown. The latter section of the book features difficult questions about child-adult relations.

The general tone of the book is one of alarm at the treatment of the worlds' children. It raises questions around the necessity of activism underscoring structural and social violence in children's experiences. However, much of the work is schematic and seems to lack an even balance in certain parts.

Stephens, S., 1995, *Children and the Politics of Culture*, New Jersey, Princeton University Press, 366 pp., including Index, ISBN: 0-691-04329-9.

Sharon Stephens (who died recently, much to the loss of child studies) was the editor of an important collection of essays on childhood in the "postmodern/post-colonial" world. Drawing on Robert Coles' (1986) assertion that the politics of nations becomes children's everyday psychology, Stephens asks how global forces affect children and how they reshape the cultural politics that characterise their lives. What visions of society and culture underlie international rights discourses? Stephens asks how the hybrid identity of some of the world's children relates to the more circumscribed perceptions of culture contained in the child rights discourse. The papers constituting the book make a theoretic and practical contribution to new ways of understanding childhood in diverse regions and contexts. Stephens examines the constructed nature of childhood culture as a theoretically and politically contested term, and the reasons why childhood and culture are contested and reshaped in contemporary contexts.

Stephens notes that the aim of the book is not to undermine international rights discourses but to make them more flexible. The UN Convention on the Rights of the Child should be used strategically and critically. Stephens suggests that global discourses have entered localities and that being the case, the study of childhood should neither be cast in a cultural relativist mould nor in a crass universalist mould. International rights discourses must neither be uncritically celebrated nor completely jettisoned. International rights can make a difference in situations where children's lives are immediately threatened, where they are subjected to torture and imprisonment, and where States oppress ethnic and religious minorities.

Part One of the book examines the disappearance of childhood, or childhood at risk, in the "new world order". The writers who contributed to this section of the book are Norma Field, with "the stresses and strains of Japanese childhood", Marilyn Ivy, who wrote about "recovering the inner-child in the late Twentieth Century America", and Mary John, who made a critical analysis of children's rights in free-market culture. (John's paper is summarised in detail in the annotated bibliography).

Norma Field's work shows how Japanese children have no free time and that most of their lives are spent in school and cram colleges even from a very young age. Fierce competition between pupils results in harsh bullying among groups of children. Because children live stressful lives in contemporary Japan, they are developing diseases usually associated with adults, such as high blood pressure. There is a high suicide rate among children in Japan. The article marks the erosion of space to dream and play, diminution of imagination, and the creation of compliant hard workers for adult life. Mothers and children within the system form what Field calls the "mother-child labouring team". Fathers spend long hours working and entertaining business partners outside the home while mothers take on the task of shaping children for their future adaptation to the adult marketplace. Field articulates the loss of childhood in Japan in capitalism as being part of a process of other forms of childhood disintegration. War and poverty in the Third World are expressions of conflicts created within the framework of capitalism, as are the "war-like" situations in which poor urban children in inner-city environments in the First World become enmeshed.

Marilyn Ivy's piece links concern in public discourse in America with missing children and child abuse with burgeoning "inner-child" psychotherapies for adults. Inner-child therapies assist adults to act as caretakers of the part of themselves neglected in childhood. As parent to the inner child, they make up for the lack of care and abuse within their own "dysfunctional" families. Although Ivy does not seek to underestimate the impact of child abuse in society, she highlights discourses on the disappearance of childhood to signal a sense of loss and threat to older categories of identity, including that of the protected child. Inner-child therapies locate social disease in the spoiling of childhood experience by dysfunctional adults. The family becomes a "toxic" field of relations in which boundaries protecting childhood are violated and where private life is colonised by market forces and consumer compulsions. Ivy points out that the ills of society become depoliticised in the sole location of blame for individual feelings of disease within families.

Part Two of the book explores linkages between children, identity and the State. Papers in this section are written by Hae-joang Cho, Sara Shiraishi, Vivienne Wee and Pamela Reynolds. They cover topics concerning school examination systems in Korea, the use of children's stories in the formation of nationalist discourse in Indonesia, children and the population policy in

Singapore, and youth and politics in South Africa. Hae-jong Cho's article is similar to that of Field on Japan as it examines the strain of preparation for examinations in Korea. Shiraishi's paper shows how appeals to tradition concerning ideas of childhood are incorporated into the formation of nation-states. Stephens (p.28) notes that in Ivy's work, while risks to children in America are depoliticised through concentration on family dysfunction as opposed to the public sphere and political economy, Shiraishi suggests that what happens to children in Indonesia is depoliticised because State education systems are couched in "timeless" cultural traditions. Pamela Reynolds' paper on youth and politics in South Africa is also summarised in detail in the annotated bibliography.

Part Three explores children and the politics of minority cultural identity. The writers in this section of the book raise important questions as to how narrowly the right to a cultural identity for children should be defined in rights discourses. Hybrid identities are a challenge to the narrow definition of culture and cultural boundaries. Kathleen Hall writes on the fluid identities of British-Sikh teenagers. Ruth Mandel, writing on the second generation children of Turkish migrants in Germany, shows how Turkish youths in Germany prefer to retain dual citizenship and to draw on both sets of identity. Manuela Carneiro da Cunha writes on childhood among Brazilian Indians and Sharon Stephens concentrates on the effects of radioactive fallout from the Chernobyl disaster on Norwegian Sami nomads and the implications of the fallout for Sami children and for the transmission of features of social life considered to be markers of Sami identity.

Part Six of the book asks questions about the recovery and reconstruction of childhood. Njabulo Ndebele, a South African writer, deals with the section on recovering childhood in the New South Africa. His paper is further summarised in detail in the annotated bibliography.

Stephens raises important questions about the collection of papers. As regards the "erosion of childhood" outlined in the work of Field, Ivy and Ndebele, she writes:

> When do deviations from the ideal form of modern childhood come to represent not just differences within the structured coherence of a globalised modernity, but also signs of the dissolution and reshaping of this system? (p. 27).

Writers on the hybrid identities of some of the world's children remind readers that young people are not necessarily put at risk by the forces of global capitalism. Their cultural repertoires may indeed be enriched by a plurality of options in terms of mixing cultural artifacts and playing with identities drawing on diverse cultural traditions. For young Turkish youths living in Germany, just as for second generation British–Sikh children, the "right to cultural identity" defined in the UN Convention on the Rights of the Child is neither possible nor desirable.

The collection describes youth creativity and suggests, in the words of one of the contributors, that "What we must guarantee for future generations is not the preservation of cultural products, but the capacity for cultural production" (Carneiro da Cunha, p. 31). He is warning us here of the ossification of culture into relics of the past and a stultifying appeal to official versions of culture.

In relation to the importance of retaining spaces of play for children, Stephens writes: "We might see play as active exploration of imagined environments built up in the spaces of existing social life. In this light, play is the ground of a notion of culture as a living resource, rather than objectified product" (p. 34). In formulating cultural rights discourses, the challenge is to facilitate through legal structures the protection of childhood and cultural differences as foundations for "deep play". However such attempts need to guard against commoditisation of play and of leisure. The retention of spaces for "deep play" allows children a critical space from which to reflect on and shape their lives.

Trones, I., C. Jenks, J. Qvortrup, I. Rizzini, B. Thorne, 1999, *Childhood: A Global Journal of Child Research. Special Issue: Understanding Child Labour* 6(1).

Childhood is a useful recent journal on child studies. Although some volumes are preoccupied with childhood in industrialised countries, Volume 6, No.1 of 1999 provides an overview of global discussions concerning child labour pertinent to studies in Africa. The issue comprises selected papers from the Urban Childhood Conference held from 9 to 12 June 1997 in Trondheim. I refer briefly to the Introduction to the journal and cover in more detail the articles of William Myers, Martin Woodhead and Ben White elsewhere in the annotated bibliography.

The journal contains varying perspectives on issues dealing with child labour. Some of the authors provide timely criticism of narrow conceptions about child labour and the politics of policy intervention in particular contexts. Agnes Camacho, Martin Woodhead, William Myers and Lisa Frederiksen write on the need for children's understanding of their work and the contexts in which it takes place, understanding that has been ignored in much campaigning against child work. In the Introduction to the volume, Per Miljeteig notes the emergence of vocal groups of working children and youths and concludes that "working children should be seen as partners and participants in the fight against their economic exploitation rather than as opponents". Miljeteig argues that Article 32 of the United Nations Convention on the Rights of the Child (CRC) expands thinking on child labour by referring to children's right to protection from economic exploitation and from hazardous work. He suggests that the article "sets the focus on the right to protection from exploitation, rather than criminalising work itself" (p. 8). He asserts the need to research the variety of children's work, for example, formal and informal work, domestic chores, work beyond regulation, within families, and family business and agriculture. Meljeteig refers to Martin Woodhead's article, suggesting that there is increasing understanding that work for many children is an inevitable and necessary part of growing up and contributing to their families and their own future prospects. Woodhead warns against a pathological model of work harming development that already dominates research. Myers argues that the CRC should not be used to emphasise reduction of children's economic activity but rather their protection from harmful work.

Other articles include one by Jonathan Blagbough and Edmund Glynn's (pp. 51-56) of Anti-Slavery International. Their article concerns child domestic work in relation to proposed international standards prohibiting the worst forms of child labour. The authors show how although legislation exists to protect children (mainly girls) from the worst forms of domestic service, it has had little impact on the lives of children working in domestic settings. They suggest that reforms could be introduced by working directly with employers of child domestic workers to oblige them to make room for some children's schooling and leisure, and the reduction of long hours of work. They stress that very little reliable and detailed knowledge exists about children in domestic work situations.

Agnes Camacho (pp. 57-73) examines the relationship between families, child work and migration in Metro Manila in the Philippines. She worked with fifty children below eighteen years of age who had come from the provinces to work as waged domestics in the capital. The children regarded the decision to work as their own but made in consultation with their families. Most of them felt impelled to work to augment family incomes. The children expressed the following wishes in relation to the government and the society: higher wages, more benefits, protection from abusive employees, appropriate education programmes and a change in society's low regard for domestic workers.

Geir Myrstad (pp. 75-88) of the International Labour Organisation writes of trade unions and child labour in a way that underscores the particular assumptions of trade unions in relation to child labour and also promotes a specific conception of family. He notes that trade unions have an interest in opposing child labour to protect work for adults. He suggests that trade unionists use their experience in negotiations and collective bargaining to include improvements for child workers in their agreements with employers. Education is offered as an antidote to child labour — a stance criticised by other writers in the volume and also by Olga Nieuwenhys (see above). Nieuwenhys further shows how banning children from work perpetuates a particular conception of family, State and institutional support to families. The forms of support to nuclear families that existed to some extent in industrialised countries do not cover marginalised groupings within those societies or to poorer countries in the Third World. Myrstad takes a positive view of the Labelling Child Labour Products Campaign, which in India resulted in the closure of children's access to textile work and worsened their economic standing by pushing them into more exploitative forms of work. The writer is a proponent of "Children in School, Adults at Work, Exploiters in Jail", a slogan that is appropriate within particular social contexts but may not be so in others.

Jim McKechine and Sandy Hobbs write of how industrialised countries are complacent about child labour in their own countries. There is no scrutiny of social conditions regarding working children in industrialised countries. The writers found in a study of children and work in Britain that mixing employment and full-time education is the norm in this country. About 50% to 79% of the sample of children between fourteen and fifteen years old had worked in the past or were working during the research period. The children did a large variety of work. The laws protecting children at work in Britain were ineffective because the majority of working children did not have work permits. The children viewed their work positively, stating that it gave them a sense of autonomy and responsibility and increased their self-esteem. The writers point to the ineffectiveness of the traditional dichotomy between "bad" and "good" child work and argue that what is viewed as good or bad work will vary cross-culturally. The authors conclude that whereas the different kinds of work done and the conditions under which they are done may vary between industrialised and developing countries, globally speaking, children as employees "have no voice; their rights are not recognised and they have little power in society" (p. 98).

Ben White (pp. 133-44) in an article entitled "Defining the Intolerable: Child work, global standards and cultural relativism", argues that the problem of child labour should be viewed from the perspective of child abuse at work, as opposed to the involvement of children in work. He suggests that organisations such as ILO deny children's agency in the negotiation of value and in the struggle to improve their own lives. Judging which work is harmful, particularly when trying to set international standards, leads to confrontation with issues concerning cultural relativism. The greater the understanding of the diversity of children's lives, the more we come to understand that child abuse and exploitation at work are not homogeneous, unitary or constant.

The author writes that while the principles of relativism are important in giving local content to global standards, they are more usefully seen as tools of discovery and understanding than uncritical legitimation of local forms of child work. The most useful form of cultural relativism then allows analysts to question the supposed universal ideas that are becoming "a way of opening eyes to the variety of human ideology and practice, but not a basis for legitimising whatever one sees when doing this" (p. 137).

While noting with caution the limited impact of previous ILO conventions on the prevention of child labour, White notes advances in more recent ILO policy prohibiting "the most intolerable forms of child labour" (adopted in 1999). Other advances he suggests are that the distinction between paid and unpaid work has been abolished, thus recognising that unpaid forms of work may be equally or more exploitative than paid work. Working children's organisations including representatives from Asia, Africa and Latin America participated in the lead up to the 1996 ILO Convention on Child Labour. White however concludes with the question, "On what basis does one decide that work is exploitative, harmful and harzardous?"

Woodhead, M., 1999, "Combating Child Labour: Listen to What the Children Say", pp. 27-49, in *Childhood: A Global Journal of Child Research*, vol. 6 (1).

Martin Woodhead summarises children's occupational preferences and their views concerning employed work and school, using a study involving 300 boys and girls aged ten to fifteen in Bangladesh, Ethiopia, the Philippines and Central America. The study was conducted by Radda Barnen

(Swedish Save the Children) and is entitled, "Children's Perspectives on their Working Lives". Woodhead refers to the notion of a continuum for grading children's work from altogether harmful, on the one hand, to altogether beneficial on the other (see Myers' article above where this idea is first presented in the annotated bibliography). In line with that notion, the 1998 ILO Conference proposed to take measures to prevent children from engaging in extremely hazardous forms of child labour. Woodhead questions whether a mechanistic continuum model can encompass more unquantifiable forms of hazard, for example, the psychological effects of harm in relation to work. Harm cannot be distilled through looking at the nature of work in isolation. Work takes place within particular socio-cultural contexts where it is attributed specific value. Children are not passive victims of physical and psychological harm at work, but are social actors negotiating with a wide variety of people including parents, employers, customers and peers in the context of work. In fact, work in many cases is an integral part of children's lives and it contributes in important ways to their identities and their sense of self.

The children generally reported a positive view of their own work in relation to the work of other children. They stressed the economic benefits of work in supporting themselves and their families. Children were able to buy items for themselves, and work also provided social contexts that were often fun. Difficulties involved children's relationships with those in authority who had power over them. In relation to school, the children outlined the positive attributes as being learning to read and write. However, only half the children in the study said that schooling improved their work prospects. Most children saw school as a place for making friends and for play. Good results could earn one self-respect and social respect in communities. The negative aspects of schooling included the cost, a loss of earnings, corporal punishment and bullying.

Combining work and school was the overwhelming preference of 77 percent of the children covered in the study. The results conceal a wide variety of situations faced by children in Bangladesh, Ethiopia, the Philippines and in Central America. In terms of the overall sample, 24 percent of children in Bangladesh and 29 percent in Ethiopia preferred working only and not going to school. Few children in these countries stated that they would like to go to school, excluding work altogether. In contrast, 17 percent of children from the Philippines study and 21 percent of children from the Central American study stated that they would like to go to school only. Few children in the latter countries said they would like to work and not to go to school. The above differences relate to the availability and economic significance of schooling in the respective countries.

Woodhead argues that within child labour discourse there is an assumption that access to schooling is the solution to the detrimental effects of child work. Woodhead concludes that school is valued by children but it is not seen as an alternative to working. His article therefore raises questions about the United Nations Convention on the Rights of the Child where work is viewed as negative and school as positive. Sixty-five percent of children saw work as a necessity and when asked what they would do if a law was passed banning all children under fifteen years from working, they said they would defy the law (p. 46). Instead of "removal" and "rehabilitation" from work children seek support and regulation of their current working situations.

Recent Conferences

Children and Youth as Emerging Categories in Post-colonial Africa, University of Leuven, Belgium, November 5-6, 1999

Some of the proceedings of the above conference are to be published. For details of the publication, contact Filip De Boeck in the Department of Cultural and Social Anthropology at Leuven University, Belgium and Alcinda Honwana, care of the Department of Social Anthropology, University of Cape Town, South Africa. Most papers were first drafts and not to be quoted, so I will outline the general themes of the conference. A list of the unpublished papers appears at the end of the section, with the institutional base of each writer, should readers be interested in following up some of the contributions.

The three major themes of the conference included children and youth in relation to political violence, identity, and marginality in varying contexts in post-colonial Africa. Contributors to the conference unanimously acknowledged the economic and political difficulties for children and youths in fragmented and disrupted social contexts. In the preamble, the organisers suggested that it is important to counter notions of the vulnerable and dependent child in Western discourse through an examination of childhood and youth in Africa. It is therefore no longer pertinent to define children and youth as passive recipients of socialisation or as incomplete adults.

They are actors contributing to the creation and shaping of social worlds in particular social and cultural contexts. The role of children in economic processes in Africa as well as their incorporation into and participation in wars needs to be acknowledged. There is emphasis on the emergence of youth cultures. Honwana and De Boeck argue that, in Africa, the integration of youth into mainstream society is severely limited. They write:

> An increasing number of children and youths seem to be excluded from education, healthcare, salaried jobs and even access to the status of adult, given the financial incapacity of many youngsters in contemporary Africa to construct a house, formally marry and raise children or reach higher education (p. 1).

Despite the above difficulties the political, cultural and economic activities that youth and children nonetheless generate in Africa are recognised as important areas of research.

The liminal status of young people on the margins of mainstream society is linked in the ideas of many with creativity and danger[9]. Liminality casts children and youth as makers and breakers of society in relation to memory, tradition and identity. An important area of consideration is how children give meaning to disruption and fragmentation. The ambivalent position that "out-of-place" youths occupy in contemporary Africa is captured in Filip De Boeck's use of the literal and metaphoric idea of borderlands, "boundaries" across which goods, people and imaginary constitutions of self flow, where social meanings and bodies are dismembered and reshaped (as is the case in the competition for diamonds on the war torn borders between Angola and Zaire).

Children, Youth and Political Conflict

Pamela Reynolds discussed the contribution of children and youths to the South African struggle. She stressed children's conscious decision to enter a liberation struggle for the sake of an envisioned future. Their role in changing South Africa has not been sufficiently recognised. Reynolds drew on her 1995 work, as reviewed above. Mats Utas presented a paper on the experience of girls and women in the Sierra Leonean liberation/civil war.

---

[9] The notion of children being potentially dangerous is not a new one and has constituted a common theme in adult conceptions about childhood and society especially when children are seen as a threat to adult systems of authority and order.

He raised questions concerning young women's agency in a social context where their survival depended on attaching themselves to a powerful military commander. Failure to do so, even if they did not particularly want to enter into a sexual relationship with a commander, resulted in systematic rape and torture. Alcinda Honwana discussed the experience of girls as war-wives in war-torn Mozambique. Rémy Bazenguissa-Ganga described youth militias in Congo showing how, prior to democratic elections, they gave protection to emerging leaders. Youth militias increasingly became perpetrators of violence in civil war. Said Adejumobi wrote of identity formation among students in Nigeria. He traced the decline in student union organisation in the 1980s due to State oppression and the increasing membership of "cult" groups. These groups were secretive and they often met at night. Each group harboured a set of beliefs that were shared with only members of the group. The groups developed harsh initiation rituals and increasingly protected their own members. Violence between groups was, therefore, not uncommon. Abubakar Momoh's paper traces marginalised youth cultures in Nigerian cities promulgated by what was known as "area boys and girls". Area boys and girls no longer attend school and are formally unemployed. Many area boys and girls are involved in petty crime and in the distribution of stolen goods and drugs. The distinction between "youth" and "adult" begins to blur within this particular cultural domain, for example, with the emergence of the "youthmen" category, men who are still affiliated to area boy culture as they are chronically unemployed and cannot fulfil obligations expected from adults. Momoh concludes that the question of youth crisis and marginalisation is linked to a further question of the social [and political] exclusion of youths from mainstream society, a characteristic of power relations in Africa. The crisis of youth is underpinned by material and ideological crises and cannot be narrowly viewed as a generational crisis.

Children, Youth and Transitions

Andy Dawes presented a paper on youth and political change in South Africa. From 1992 to 1996, Dawes and Finchilescue conducted a study of children between fourteen and seventeen years from population groups demarcated by apartheid as Black African, White, Coloured and Indian. They sought to gauge the children's contemporary socio-political ideas in relation to sub-national identifications and concluded that the racial divisions that are a legacy of apartheid continue to have salience in the

ideas expressed by young people. In 1996, most children from Coloured,
White and Indian groupings predicted long-term deterioration in the
country. In contrast, Black Africans were largely positive about political
changes. Youths have therefore not uniformly embraced change in South
Africa and the tensions between population groupings may manifest
themselves in the future.

Children, Youth and Identity Formation

Steven Van Wolputte presented a paper about bachelors in charge of cattle
care among the pastoral OvaHimba in Namibia. He described how these
youths are well placed to facilitate communication between homesteads
because of their movements in grazing cattle. In addition, they have the
greatest communication with the outside world. As intermediaries between
homesteads and urban environments, they enjoy the liberty of eclectically
picking from "traditional" and "modern" ways and are able to model their
own identities in response to current changes. Wolputte writes of young
men in OvaHimba society that they embody "the many faces (or identities)
of the intermediate, or of brokerage and agency" (p. 22). Danielle Jonckers'
paper describes the relative autonomy of Bamana children in Mali, an
autonomy that reduces parent/adolescent crises. She examines the ways in
which children form their own cult associations, mirroring adult cult
associations that facilitate collective communication between people and
gods. In a study among the Gusii of South-west Kenya, Stella Okemwa
describes how contemporary change is triggered by demographic, political
and economic crises. The cultural functionality of land, as a place of
belonging and as a resource distributed in terms of bonds of affiliation, is
being disrupted. Children are ambivalently perceived, more traditionally, as
a source of wealth, but also as mediating and hindering access to resources.
The paper follows — in a context of dwindling resources — the story of a
boy, Gichana, born out of wedlock and marginalised by both his biological
father's kin and his mother's kin after her departure in marriage. Gichana
forges for himself a sense of belonging beyond the family with other young
people who share a similar sense of rejection. He is later acknowledged as
the founder of an agnatic line through marriage and the symbolic incorporation
of his children into his grandfather's agnatic line by his grandmother. His
early death clarifies his position as an outsider, however, as his mother's
brothers refuse his burial on ancestral land. Neither do they fulfil
obligations towards his widow

Children and Youths Out of Place

Michael Barret reviews routes through childhood to adulthood for Mbunda men and women in rapidly changing social conditions in Zamibia. In conventional contexts, personhood is granted to adults. Adulthood is connected with rights, obligations and associated behaviour, the attainment of cultural heritage, and respect. Within this framework, youths are viewed as incomplete adults and they occupy a marginal position in society. Youths, however, find ways of informally ridiculing village elders and of asserting a space of alterity. The paper shows how Mbunda youths manage to create coherent lives for themselves despite the conflicting demands of changing socio-economic realities and local cultural models of adulthood.

Filip De Boeck writes on the ambivalent status of young men, *bana lunda*, from Zaire involved in diamond mining in the eastern border regions of Angola. He uses the notion of borderlands, frontiers with their multiple contemporary meanings, to create a rich metaphoric matrix in which to view the position of migrant youth (boys and girls). The idea of borderlands accommodates the two-way interchange between global and local influences and exchange. For example, the tropes of hunting and gathering and the warrior are utilised in contexts of frontier urbanisation. Identities here are ambivalent, contextual, negotiable and polysemic. The pursuit of wealth in a violent and dangerous context is linked to ideas that wealth must be hunted down, trapped and tamed. Sources of wealth, such as game, are unpredictable and dangerous. In the border region, discourses on the negation of social ideals including witchcraft, cannibalism, incest and homosexuality are linked to the successful mining of diamonds and their danger. Anti-social sacrifices and practices have to be undertaken to ensure wealth. Young people working in the border regions therefore espouse ambivalent identities where opposites flow into one another and exchange meanings — for instance, inside-outside; the wild bush in contrast to the social order of the village; notions of what is marginal and what is central, young people as killers and life-givers, and as generators of violence and weavers of social networks.

Papers

Contact details are given where they were provided. Readers are referred to the conference organisers for more details.

Abdullah, I., 1999, (An untitled paper on lumpen youth and their participation in the RUF operations in Sierra Leone, E-mail: iabdullah@unwc.ac.za).

Adejumobi, S., 1999, *From Unionism to Cultism: Students and Identity Recomposition in Nigeria's Tertiary Institutions,* Unpublished paper. (Department of Political Science, Lagos State University. E-mail: b.ahonsi@fordfound.org).

Banda, G. and Oxfam, 1991, *Adjusting to Adjustment in Zambia: Women and Young People's Responses to a Changing Economy,* Oxford. Oxfam Publications.

Barrett, M., 1999, *The Changing Face of Adulthood: Mbunda Youth and Personhood in Western Zambia,* Unpublished paper (Department of Cultural Anthropology and Ethnography, Uppsala University).

Bazenguissa-Ganga. R., 1999, *Les milices politiques du Congo: propositions pour une approche des dynamiques internes de la globalisation,* Ms (Centre d'Études d'Afrique Noire (CEAN), L'Ecole des Hautes Études en Sciences Sociales, Paris. E-mail: bazengui@ehess.fr).

Dawes, A. and G. Finchilescu, 1999, *Youth and Political Change: The Case of South Africa,* Unpublished paper (Department of Psychology University of Cape Town. E-mail: dawes@psipsy.uct.ac.za).

De Boeck, F., 1999, *Borderland Breccia: The Mutant Hero in the Historical Imagination of a Central African Diamond Frontier,* Unpublished paper (Department of Cultural and Social Anthropology, University of Leuven. Belgium, E-mail: filip.deboeck@ant.kuleuven.ac.be).

Honwana, A., 1999, *Untold War Stories: Young Women and War in Mozambique Department of Social Anthropology,* University of Cape Town, Unpublished paper (Department of Social Anthropology, University of Cape Town. E-mail: honwana@beattie.uct.ac.za).

Jonckers, D., 1999, *How is it Possible to be a Bamana Child Today? Identity Formation in South Mali,* Unpublished paper.

Momoh, A., 1999, *The Youth Crisis in Nigeria: Understanding the Phenomenon of the Area Boys and Girls,* Unpublished paper (Department of Political Studies, Lagos State University). E-mail: soa@alpha.linkserv.com.

Okemwa, S., 1999, *Sugar Babies and Teenage Grandfathers: A Case Study on Youth Strategies in a Quest for Descent Affiliation and Ancestral Continuity*, Unpublished paper.

Utas, M., 1999, *An Agency of Victims: Young Women's Surviving Strategies in the Liberation Civil War,* Unpublished paper (Department of Cultural anthropology and Ethnology, Uppsala University).

Van Wolputte, S., 1999, *The Beeswax Rifle: Youngsters as Messengers and Heralds of the Old and the New Among the Ovahimba of Northern Namibia,* Unpublished paper (Department of social and Cultural Anthropology, University of Leuven, Belgium. E-mail: Steven.Vanwolputte@ant.kuleuven.ac.be).

Understanding Exclusion, Creating Value: African Youth in a Global Age, July 30-31, 1999, Cape Town, South Africa

Proceedings of the above conference are to be produced in a publication. For information regarding the publication, please contact Jean Comaroff, Department of Anthropology, University of Chicago, E-mail: jcomarof@midway.uchicago.edu.

The themes of the conference included: globalisation and youth: Africa in comparative perspective; the political economics of youth marginalisation; State, socialisation and education; youth culture and mass media; activism, violence and criminalisation; research on youth policy and "interventions"; young scholars and youth research; mapping research on African youth, forging networks; and towards an integrated research and training programme.

The conference opened with a set of statements on youth by Peter Kopoka, Institute of Development Studies, University of Dar Es-Salaam; Richard Mkandawire, Centre for Youth Studies, The University of Venda; Penina Mlama, Executive Director of the Forum for African Women; Sudhir Venkatesh, Society of Fellows, Columbia University; Abubakar Momoh, Department of Political Studies, Lagos State University; Barthelemy Kuate-Defo, Department of Demographics, University of Montreal; Zolani Ngwane, Department of Anthropology, University of Chicago; Prem Naidoo, Director of the National Research Foundation, Pretoria; and Jean and John Comarof, Department of Anthropology, University of Chicago. The themes addressed included the political economics of youth marginalisation (Kopoka); placating and cajoling a de-Africanised youth (Mkandawire); the crisis of educational institutions in Africa and the vulnerability of female youth (Mlama); a comparative look at inner-city youth in America (Venkatesh); activism, violence and criminalisation of youth in Africa (Momoh); marginalisation and reproductive health (Kuate-Defo);

State, education and the politics of youth (Ngwane); the education and training system in South Africa (Naidoo); and globalisation and youth (J. and J. Comaroff).

A number of papers and books on youth issues published by participants formed a background to the colloquium. Those that do no appear in the annotated bibliography already, or in Fiona Ross' annotated bibliography on children, are now listed.

Papers and Books

Bazenguissa-Ganga, R., 1999, "The Spread of Political Violence in Congo Brazzaville", *African Affairs*, Vol.98, pp. 37-54.

Diawara, M., 1998, "Chantier De Champs: La jeune génération de l'aire culturelle mande face aux traditions orales", pp. 197-216, in B. Jewsiewick and J. Létourneau (eds.) *Septentrion. Identités en Mutation. Socialité en germination.* Sillery (Quebec): Les éditions du Septentrion. ISBN: 2-89448-126-8.

Jewsiewicki, B and J. Létourmeau (eds.), 1998, *Presentation*, pp. 7-23, in *Les Jeunes à l'ére de la mondialisation: Quête identitaire et conscience historique*, Sillery (Quebec): Les éditions du Septentrion, ISBN: 2-89448-125-X.

Kopoka, P. A., 1998, *Poverty and Youth Unemployment in Tanzania.* Paper presented to the Seventeenth Annual Scientific Conference and General Meeting, Mkonge Hotel, Tanga, Tanzania 23-26 November.

Mkandawire, R. M., 1999, *Experiences in Youth Policy and Programme Development in Commonwealth Africa.*

Momoh, A., 1998, *Area Boys and the Nigerian Political Crisis.* Paper prepared for the workshop on Manoeuvring in an Environment of Uncertainty, Vadstena, Sweden, June 3-5 (Draft).

Nsamenang, A. B., 1993, *Reflection on Human Development and Social Intervention in Africa*, in *UNESCO Africa*, N°17, pp. 98-105.

Ngwane, Z., 1999, "Real Men Re-awaken their Fathers' Homesteads. The Educated Leave them in Ruins": The Articulation of Two Modes of Social Reproduction in Post-Apartheid Rural South Africa. Unpublished paper, Department of Anthropology, University of Chicago.

Venkatesh, S. A. and S. Levitt, 1999, *The Political Economy of an American Street Gang*, Unpublished paper, Society of Fellows, Harvard University and Department of Economics, Harvard University.

A Few Web-sites on Child Studies

www.lib.uct.ac.za/eresources
http://biblioline.nisc.can/help/products/qcan/doc/canintro.htm
www.nisc.com

Additional References

Some of the references listed below were not properly referenced at source.

Abdullah, I. and P. Muana, 1998, *The Revolutionary Front of Sierra Leone: A Revolt of the Lumpen Proletariat,* in C. Clapham (ed.), *African Guerillas,* London, James Currey.

Anker, R. and H. Melkas, 1996, *Economic Incentives for Children and Families to Eliminate or Reduce Child Labour,* Geneva, International Labour Organisation, Labour Market Policies Branch.

Addison, T., S. Bhalotra, F. Coutter and C. Heady, 1997, *Child Labour in Pakistan and Ghana*: A Comparative Study, First Draft, Bath, Centre for Development Studies, University of Bath.

Banard, D. (ed.), 1997, *The Youth Book: A Directory of South African Youth Organisations, Service Providers and Resource Material,* Pretoria, Human Sciences Research Council (HSRC).

Bazenguissa-Ganga, R., 1996, "Milices politiques et bandes armées à Brazzaville", *Les Études du CERI,* Vol. 13.

Bazenguissa-Ganga, R., 1998, "Instantanés au coeur de la violence: Anthropologie de la victime au Congo-Brazzaville", pp. 150-152, *Cahiers d'Études Africaines.*

Bazenguissa-Ganga, R., 1999, "La Popularisation de la violence politique au Congo", *Politique Africaine,* Vol. 73.

Blomqvist, U., 1995, *Protection of Children in Refugee Emergencies: The Importance of Early Social Work Intervention — The Rwanda Experience,* Stockholm, Radda Barnen.

Bonnet, C., 1995, *La Violence comme Arme de Guerre au Rwanda: Du silence à la reconnaissance,* Paris, Fondation de France.

Boyden, J. and Myers W. E., 1995, *Exploring Alternative Approaches to Combating Child Labour: Case Studies from Developing Countries,* Florence, UNICEF/ Innocenti Occasional Paper 8.

Boyden, J. and S. Gibbs, 1996, *Vulnerability and Resilience: Perceptions and Responses to Psychological Distress in Cambodia,* Oxford, INTRAC.

Boyden, J. and S. Gibbs, 1997, *Children and War. Understanding Psychological Distress in Cambodia,* Geneva, The United Nations.

Boyden, J., B. Ling and W. Meyers, 1998, *What Works for Working Children,* Stockholm, Radda Barnen, UNICEF.

Boyden, J. and D. Levison, 1999, *Children as Economic and Social Actors in the Development Process,* ms.

Chole, E., 1992, *Children of War in the Horn of Africa: The Bitter Harvest of Armed Conflict in Ethiopia, Sudan, Somalia and Djibouti,* Addis Ababa, Inter-Africa Group.

Coalition to Stop the Use of Child Soldiers, 1998, *Stop Using Child Soldiers!* London, Radda Barnen on behalf of the International Save the Children Alliance, ISBN: 2-940217-05-X.

Cruise O'Bryan, D., 1996, "The Lost Generation? Youth Identity and State Decay in Western Africa', in R. P. Werbner and T.O. Ranger (eds.) *Post-colonial Identities in Africa,* London, Zed Books.

Davin, A., 1982, "Child Labour: The Working Class Farm and Domestic Ideology in 19th Century Britain", *Development Change* 13(4), pp. 663-52.

Dawes, A., 1996, "Helping, Coping and Cultural Healing", in *Recovery. Research and Co-operation on Violence, Education and Rehabilitation of Young People,* vol. 1(5).

Dawes, A. and A. Honwana, 1996, "Children, Culture and Mental Health: Interventions in Conditions of War", pp. 74-81, in B. Efraime Júnior *et al.* (eds.) Children War and Persecution — Rebuilding Hope: Proceedings of the Congress in Mozambique 1-4 December, Maputo, *Rebuilding Hope.*

De Smedt, J., 1998, "Child Marriages in Rwandan Refugee Camps' *Africa,* Vol. 68(2): 211-37.

Dodge, C. P. and M. Raundalen, (eds.), 1987, *War, Violence and Children in Uganda,* Oslo, Norwegian University Press.

Dodge, C. P., 1991, *National and Societal Implications of War on Children,* pp.11f, in Dodge, C.P. & M. Raundalen (eds.) *Reaching Children in War: Sudan, Uganda and Mozambique,* Uppsala, Sigma Forlag.

Dube, L., 1998, *Surviving in the Streets: The Survival Techniques of Street Children in Harare,* with special reference to parking boys, Unpublished paper presented at the Academic Research Seminar on Children. University of Zimbabwe, 30-31 July.

Efraime Júnior, B., P. Riedesser, J. Walter, H. Adam, and P. Steudtner (eds.) 1996, "Children, War and Persecution — Rebuilding Hope: Proceedings of the Congress in Maputo, Mozambique 1-4 December", Maputo, Special Volume of *Rebuilding Hope*.

FAO, 1996, *Report of the Study on the Nutritional Impact of Armed Conflicts on Children*, Food and Nutrition Division, United Nations Food and Agriculture Organisation, Rome.

Feinstein International Famine Center, 1998, *Children and Adolescents in Violent Societal Change* (UNHCR and Tufts University workshop). Medford, Mass.: Alan Shawn Feinstein International Famine Center.

Fuglesang, M., 1994, "Veils and Videos: Female Youth Culture on the Kenya Coast", Stockholm, *Stockholm Studies in Social Anthropology*.

Gondola, C. D., 1998, "Dream and Drama: The Search for Elegance Among Congolese Youth", *African Studies Review*, Vol.41 (2).

Goodwin, M. H., 1990, *He-Said-She-Said: Talk as Social Organisation Among Black Children*, Bloomington, Indiana, Indiana University Press.

Green, E. C. and M. G. Wessells, 1995, *Evaluation of the Mobile War Trauma Team: Program on Meeting the Psychological Needs of Children in Angola*. Richmond, Virginia: Christian Children's Fund.

Grootaart, C. and H. Patrinos, 1998, *The Policy Analysis of Child Labour: A Comparative Study*, Unpublished working paper, Washington DC: World Bank.

Gough, D., 1996, "Defining the Problem", *Child Abuse and Neglect*, Vol. 20 (11): 993-1002.

Gupta, L., 1996, *Exposure to War-related Violence Among Rwandan Children and Adolescents: A Brief Report on the National Baseline Trauma Survey*, Rwanda, UNICEF Trauma Recovery Programme.

Kurimoto, E., and S. Simonse (eds.), 1998, *Conflict, Age and Power in North-East Africa*, London, James Currey.

Lachman, P., 1996, "Child Protection in Africa: The Road Ahead", *Child Abuse and Neglect*, vol. 20(7), pp. 543-547.

Lancy, D., 1996, *Playing on Mother-Ground. Cultural Routines for Children's Development*, New York, Guilford Press.

Lowicki, J., 1999, *Emergency and Post-Emergency Reconstruction: Setting an Agenda for Adolescents*, Report prepared for the Women's Commission for Refugee Women and Children.

Human Rights Watch-Africa and Human Rights Watch-Children's Rights Project, 1994, *Sudan, The Lost Boys: Child Soldiers and Unaccompanied Boys in Southern Sudan*, vol. 6(10).

Ingleby, D., 1985, "Professionals as Socializers: The 'Psy Complex'", pp. 79 109, in S. Spitzer and A. T. Scull (eds.), *Research in the Law, Deviance and Social Control: A Research Annual*, Vol. 7, London, JAI Press.

International Labour Organisation, 1988, *Conditions of Work Digest: The Emerging Response to Child Labour*, 7(1), Geneva, ILO.

International Labour Organisation 1991, *Conditions of Work Digest, Child Labour, Law and Practice*, 10(1), Geneva, ILO.

International Labour Organisation 1996, *Child Labour: Targeting the Intolerable*, Geneva, ILO.

International Labour Organisation 1998, *Proposed New International Labour Standards on Extreme Forms of Child Labour*, Geneva, ILO.

Ishengoma, A. K. and G. Nchahaga, 1995, *Child Labour in Plantations in Tanzania*, Dar Es Salaam, ILO.

Knaul, F., 1995, *Young workers, Street Life and Gender: The Effect of Education and Work Experience on Earnings in Colombia*, Unpublished Master's dissertation, Harvard University, Cambridge.

Kurimoto, E. and S. Simonse, 1998, *Conflict, Age and Power in North East Africa*, London, James Currey.

Levinson, D., 1991, *Children's Labour Force Activity and Schooling in Brazil*. Unpublished dissertation, University of Michigan.

Levinson, D., R. Anker, S. Ashrat and S. Barge, 1996, *Is Child Labour Really Necessary in India's Carpet Industry?* Labour Market Paper 15, Geneva, ILO.

Mkandawire, R., 1996, *Training Programmes for Youth in Commonwealth Africa: Is There Room for the Girl Child?* Commonwealth Youth Programme Africa Centre.

Nardinelli, C., 1990, *Child Labour and the Industrial Revolution*. Bloomington, Indiana, Indiana University Press.

Ndima, C. T., 1995, *Girls' Primary Education in Rural Areas, with Reference to Dropouts: A case study of Tarime District*, Master's dissertation, University of Dar Es-Salaam.

Oloko, B. A., 1991, "Children's Work in Urban Nigeria: A Case Study of Young Lagos Traders", in W. E. Myers (ed.), *Protecting Working Children*, London, ZED Books/UNICEF.

Reynolds, P., 1995, *Making the World Mindful of the Pain of the Young*, unpublished paper, Department of Social Anthropology, University of Cape Town.

Robinson, S. and L. Biersteker, 1997, *First Call: The South African Children's Budget*, Cape Town, Institute for Democracy in South Africa (IDASA) and Youth Development Trust.

Rwebangira, M. K. and R. Liljeström (eds.), 1998, *Haraka Haraka...Look Before You Leap: Youth at the Crossroads of Custom and Modernity*, Oslo, Nordiska Afrikainstitutet.

Save the Children, 1998, "Programme Learning Group", February 26-27, Harare, Zimbabwe, *Children in Crisis*, Vol. 1, Washington, Save the Children.

Straker, G., M. Mendelsohn, F. Moosa and P. Tudin, 1996, "Violent Political Contexts and Emotional Concerns of Township Youth", *Child Development*, Vol.67, pp. 46-54.

Straker, G. and F. Moosa, 1996, "Child Soldiers in South Africa: Past, Present and Future Perspectives", pp. 51-60, in B. Efraime Júnior *et al.* (eds.) Children, War and Persecution — Rebuilding Hope: Proceedings of the Congress in Maputo, Mozambique 1-4 December, Maputo, Special edition of *Rebuilding Hope*.

Shanahan, P., 1998, *The Alternative Africa: Street Children in Accra, Ghana*, unpublished paper presented at the Academic Research Seminar on Children, University of Zimbabwe, 30-31 July.

Sharp, L. A., forthcoming. Girls, Sex and Dangers of Urban Schooling in Coastal Madagascar, in G. Bond and N. Gibson (eds.) *Contested Terrains and Constructed Categories: Contemporary Africa in Focus*, (publisher unknown).

Sharp, L. A., 1999, *A Children's Independence: Marching Towards Liberty in Coastal Madagascar*, Unpublished manuscript.

Sommers, M., 1998a, *Educating Children during Emergencies: A View From the Field*, Ms prepared for the Women's Commission for Refugee Women and Children, New York.

Sommers, M., 1998b, *A Child's Nightmare: Burundian Children At Risk: A Field Report Assessing the Protection and Assistance Needs of Burundian Children and Adolescents*, New York, Women's Commission for Refugee Women and Children.

Tine, N. D. and J. Ennew, 1998, *The African Contexts of Children's Rights. Seminar Report,* London, Global Gutter Press for Childwatch International. Oslo and CODESRIA, Senegal, ISBN: 1 901973 00 4.

Thomas, A., 1990, "Violence and Child Detainees", in B. McKendrick and W. Hoffman, (eds.), *People and Violence in South Africa,* Cape Town. Oxford University Press.

Toungara, J. M., 1995, "Generational Tensions in the Parti Démocratique de Côte d'Ivoire", *African Studies Review,* vol. 38 (2).

Track Two, Vol. 7(3) October 1998, *Bringing Youth in from the Margins.* Cape Town, Centre for Conflict Resolution, University of Cape Town.

Walvin, J., 1982, *A Child's World: A Social History of English Childhood 1800-1914,* Harmondsworth, UK, Penguin.

White, B., 1994, *Children, Work and "Child Labour": Changing Responses to Empowerment of Children,* The Hague, Institute of Social Studies.

White, B., 1996, "Globalisation and the Child Labour Problem", *Journal of International Development,* Vol. 8(6), pp. 829-39.

Women's Commission for Refugee Women and Children, March 26-April 16, 1997, *The Children's War: Towards Peace in Sierra Leone,* New York.

Wondimu, H. (ed.), 1996, *Research Papers on the Situation of Children and Adolescents in Ethiopia,* Kindernothilfe.

Woodhead, M., 1998, *Children's Perspectives on their Working Lives* Stockholm. Radda Barnen.